Four Square and the Politics of Sixth Grade Lunch

Arthur Goldman

National Middle School Association
Westerville, OH

Five lines of "Define Teacher" were originally published in an article titled "Come September" in the Winter 2005 (29.2) edition of *Ascent*. Reprinted with permission.

"Swimming Lessons" was originally published in the January 2006 (87.5) issue of *Phi Delta Kappan* and reprinted in the March 2006 (71.7) issue of *The Educational Digest*. Adapted with permission from Phi Delta Kappa International.

"The Problem with Polenta" was originally published as "The Fish Question" in the January-February 2005 (36.3) issue of *Teachers & Writers*. Adapted with permission.

"The Bus Ride into Straight Culture" was originally published as "Dear Families" in the Summer 2004 (10.1) edition of *In the Family*. Adapted with permission.

"The Contents of My Backpack" was originally published in the December 2004 (86.4) issue of *Phi Delta Kappan*. Adapted with permission.

Library of Congress Cataloging-in-Publication Data

Goldman, Steven, 1964-
  Four square and the politics of sixth grade lunch / Arthur Goldman.
      p. cm.
  ISBN 978-1-56090-241-6
  1. Middle school teaching–United States. I. Title.
  LB1623.5.G65 2011

  373.1102–dc22

                                        2010045767

National Middle School Association
4151 Executive Parkway, Suite 300
Westerville, Ohio 43081
1-800-528-NMSA f: 614-895-4750
www.nmsa.org

Once in a workshop someone suggested that we see our most challenging students as our angels because they make us change what we do and force us to learn to teach better.

This book is dedicated to my angels.

Acknowledgements

I can't begin to thank everyone who has had a part in this book. I owe a huge debt of gratitude to all of my mentors and colleagues, magazine editors who had a role in individual essays, and, of course, to the students who made it worth showing up for work every day. Because this project began as my MFA thesis, I would be particularly remiss if I didn't mention Doug Whynott, my advisor, who encouraged and inspired me to write nonfiction. I would like to thank Carla Weiland at National Middle School Association (NMSA), whose energy and enthusiasm is amazing and without whom there would not be a book. I would also like to thank Cheri Howman at NMSA for assisting in content editing and proofreading. A special thanks to Bill Ivey for his generous comments in the Foreword. And, as always, I am incredibly grateful to my family who are always so supportive —you are the best, and I love you.

Contents

Foreword by Bill Ivey ix

Preface: The Extraordinary Ordinary xi

Opening Day 1

The Contents of My Backpack 7

Why I Show Up 21

Four Square and the Politics of Sixth Grade Lunch 35

Sir Judith of the Lunchables™
and the Homework Crisis 53

The Problem with Polenta 75

Reflections from Walden Pond 87

The Bus Ride to Straight Culture 105

Swimming Lessons 117

Define teacher 127

Foreword

When I was growing up, one of the most popular games in my neighborhood was four square, a game played with a playground ball. In four square, you try to advance to the top spot as people above you get knocked out by whatever set of rules the group has agreed to. Merely mentioning the game does not necessarily transport me back to my childhood. But Arthur Goldman's description of it as "a ruthless game of politics" brought everything back so vividly that I could feel the pebbled surface of the ball, and smell its faint rubbery odor. As Mr. Goldman might have predicted, winning at four square was never my real goal. I simply wanted to be in the top two squares with my friend Phil, collaborating almost telepathically in decisions about who might be allowed to advance and how long we might allow them to stay in the third-highest square before knocking them out. Somehow, without ever having known Phil or me, Mr. Goldman knew how we thought. Such are his acute powers of observation and deep understanding of young adolescents.

Goldman sees clearly not just what is on the surface but also what lies beneath. Lunch dynamics as a study in fractals. The difference between normal sixth grade tears and 8:10-in-the-morning tears. The shift in a student's smile over time as he learns about himself, as he gains insight into what he really knows, and as he begins to earn the confidence expressed so blithely at the beginning of the year.

With simple directness and an honesty that is, by turns, moving, healing, and ultimately affirming, he takes us into his world. In so doing, he reminds us of the fundamental importance of getting to know our students as people, of teasing out and sorting through their needs, and of struggling to find the best way to meet those needs. As our country accelerates toward the indefensible and incomprehensible goal of increasing test scores above all else, we have a deep need for this reminder, whether to lead us gently back to the right path or to remind us we're not alone out there. And we will leave the book knowing, as Mr. Goldman does, that it is the little moments that define who we are, what we do, and, ultimately, why we show up.

Bill Ivey
Stoneleigh-Burnham School
October 21, 2010

Preface:
The Extraordinary Ordinary

Two months before I began my first teaching job, I received a letter from a close friend. My latest letter to her had been a greeting followed by several pages of angst—a complete catalog of the uncertainties and fears precipitated by my acceptance of a job teaching Latin in a middle school. I had reasons for being nervous. I had no formal experience, no formal training, and, the truth was, I didn't really know Latin very well. I had graduated with a major in Classics, but for me, that was mostly Greek. While Greek and Latin are both classical languages, they aren't the same. Being a good reader and knowing me well, she ignored everything in the letter, save one line. I seem to have written something like, "In one month I will become a Latin teacher." She loved the idea that the change would happen all at once, as if I could have just as easily become a duck.

No matter what the contract said, I didn't become
a Latin teacher on the first day of school. Nor did I
become a duck.

I have been involved in the teaching of adolescents now
for most of my adult life. The word *adolescent* and the
word *adult* share a common root. *Adolescent* is derived
from the present participle of *adolescere*: to grow. An
adolescent is someone who is growing. The past participle
of the same verb is *adultus*: literally, one who has grown.
Although the distinction may be etymologically accurate,
it doesn't quite describe my experience as an adult
working with adolescents. I am not a finished product.
One of the best and most painful parts of working in
middle schools is that it has required me to continue to
grow, change, and learn.

These essays are about that process of growing,
changing, and learning. I'd like to think of this collection
as a résumé in the original meaning of that word: a
 summing up. Unlike a bulleted list people draft to show
to employers, this résumé endeavors to represent the
day-to-day life in the classroom. As a consequence, it
favors the small victories over the larger accomplishments
and the important failures over the catalog of achievements.
Much of the best and most important of what happens at
school fits in the category of the extraordinary ordinary—
events too small to merit mention in even the longest
curriculum vitae.

Despite the retrospective nature of the material, much of
the action has been rendered in the present tense. I prefer

the present tense for these essays because most of them developed from the journals I kept at the time, and I wanted to preserve the sense of who I was then without employing the benefit of hindsight. This choice has also resulted in some very interesting anachronisms. Who waits for film to develop anymore? What school in this age of allergies allows a teacher to keep a jar of peanut butter for emergency lunches? There was a time when I could tell students that they had to hug me goodbye at the end of the year, but as healthy and nonthreatening as those hugs were, I'm not sure I would do that today.

I have chosen the essay form rather than a more narrative approach because I really wasn't trying to tell, what seems to me, the rather boring story of my life. Rather, as Emily Fox Gordon explains the impulse, "What I really wanted to do was to examine my experience, to think aloud." As a consequence, however, the thematic presentation of the material makes the vagaries of my career almost impossible to follow. I have worked in public schools, charter schools, independent schools, and supplementary programs. I have taught at the university level and have spent time as an administrator and as an academic coach. In many of these settings, small class sizes; multiple-year course sequences; and assistance from a string of gifted, enthusiastic interns and student teachers have made it possible for me to get to know my students well. It angers me that the most basic element of education, the opportunity to really get to know our students, is still considered a luxury in so many schools where teachers face overcrowded classrooms, unreasonable work loads, and constant pressure to quantify learning. I know I have been very lucky. But despite having taught in some great schools with great administrators, great parents, and unbelievably great students, I still found this job just plain hard sometimes. Even if all of our schools were well-run and well-funded, teaching middle school would still be a challenging profession. I think that is one of the things that draws such terrific people into the field.

This is a work of nonfiction. All of the students, teachers, and situations are presented to the best of my memory, although the context is sometimes simplified for narrative purposes. I have also changed the names and descriptions of almost everyone to respect privacy. When a student appears in more than one essay, he or she retains the same pseudonym. None of the students are composites, but over the years, sometimes my recollections of individuals have become a little fuzzy. I have done my best to reconstruct conversations and situations as accurately as possible, but I have had to employ some liberties to maintain the flow of the essays.

Years ago, I worked in a school at the foot of Beacon Hill in Boston that was close enough to my house that I could walk to work. If my timing were right, I would emerge onto Beacon Street to see the loading of the busses in front of the Bull & Finch Pub, the famous setting for the television series *Cheers*. First was a plain-looking yellow school bus transporting the well-to-do offspring of the neighborhood to a tony suburban private day school. The students wore blue and green uniforms: plaid skirts for the girls and a somewhat incongruous school baseball cap

that appeared to be a mandatory accoutrement.
They would arrive according to their family dynamics—
some holding a parent or guardian's hand; others trailing
their backpacks like tails; and a few walking beside their
adults, clearly pretending that this embarrassment was
unrelated to them.

The second bus was for dogs. Some enterprising person
offered daily dog sitting in a non-downtown location and
used a refitted mini school bus to transport them. I once
met a woman who used the service; she enthused about
the spa-like setting with fenced outdoor space and a den
furnished in doggie beds and old couches. The dogs sat in
their bus seats, much like the children would if they were
better behaved, and looked out the windows. They looked
happier than the students. Many of the families seemed
to use both services, loading their progeny and pets onto
their respective transports every morning.

Although I'm sure the kids had very different days than
the canines, I wonder how their moods compared as
they headed home. If both could speak, would they use
similar adjectives? Would they describe their days as fun?
Productive? Worth the trip?

And I often wondered, as I made my way home, about
my own day. Had my sixth graders accomplished anything
substantive, or would it have been equally worthwhile to
sit on couches, socialize, and run around a fenced yard?

On some level, I have to believe that what I do as a
teacher has meaning. It may not always be important.

There is little that one can point to on an average day and say, "Look here, this made a difference." What value there is lies more in the continuity. Each day is a small step— sometimes forward, sometimes not. How I react when no one has a pencil, when lunch conversation veers out of control, or when a student is late creates a certain environment, a structure that either contributes to learning or detracts from it. Sometimes it is hard to live in a world where the sum total of what I do may have impact, but the actual life in the classroom is full of only small moments. On other days, it feels like an odd gift—perhaps not what I asked for, sometimes damned confounding, but never boring and never without its rewards.

Opening Day

When they arrive on the first day of school, the students find their teacher on the floor rolling newspapers. All the tables have all been pushed to the back of the room, all the chairs are stacked, leaving a wide expanse of the mustard-colored carpet disturbed only by several piles of old newspapers that I have spent the last two months collecting. The room seems larger without all the furniture; not that it looks much like a classroom anyway. After several years of failed attempts to create thematically decorated classrooms, I have developed a dislike for construction paper and bulletin boards and have opted, this year, to make my classroom look as much like a living room as possible. There is a large armchair in the front, next to a small Walmart pedestal upon which sits my coffee cup. There is a trash-picked sectional at the back of the room, complete with coffee table. I have hung my father's collection of banners from the 1940s on one wall, along with various paintings that used to hang in my former bachelor days, now deemed by my wife too ugly for our home. I think the ambience is comfortable yet almost bland, like a hotel conference room, but some of my colleague's comments have been less charitable.

My new class arrives in twos and threes as their carpools or buses drop them off. They enter the room tentatively, not because of my decorating but because they know that this is not how the first day of school should start. They should be finding their seats, ready to receive their books and review the classroom rules. I smile, show them how to roll the newspaper into tubes, and hand them a stack to work on. I know most of them by name already because I taught them math last year, so there are only a few new students I need to introduce myself to. The rest know me as a math teacher and don't seem too sure about what to make of me as their homeroom teacher, now responsible for English and social studies as well as math. The strangeness of the situation has muted their voices, and the only sounds are the rustling of the paper and a few whispers. The sound of excited anticipation.

I love this particular project. I have used it as an opener for a number of classes, even as a mini-course for summer programs. I adapted it from an article I read in a math journal seven or eight years ago. It is part math, part physics, part cooperative learning, and a little imagination. We will spend a good half day on it today.

When it looks like we have a sufficient number of tubes to begin, I stand up. I don't have to ask them to look up and listen; I have their attention. This is a wonderful moment, because I know it will not be nearly so easy to create this kind of focus from here on in.

"Hi. Welcome back. Over the next couple of days we will go over class stuff, but all you need to know right now is that in the case of a fire alarm we line up silently at the door, turn off the lights and walk down the stairs to the right and line up on the sidewalk in front of the school. If we can't go to the right for some reason, there is a back stairway to the left. Any questions?"

There aren't any questions.

"In a moment, I will divide you into groups. Your group will make a structure out of these tubes you have been rolling. There are only a few rules. First: the structure must be freestanding. That means that we should be able to pick it up and move it anywhere in the room, and it should still stand. Second, you can only use the newspaper and tape, but the tape can only be used to connect paper tubes, not as a building material in itself. You can't make your structure out of tape. Third: everyone in your group must participate both in the planning and the building. Finally: The structure you build must be big enough to contain me."

With that, the students are divided into groups, and they start planning and constructing. Building a structure out of newspaper large enough to contain a 5-foot-6-inch teacher is actually a little challenging. They quickly learn that the tubes won't bear weight once they are bent. Most figure out that tripods are the easiest way to get tubes to stand, but the newspaper sheets don't make long enough tubes for the job. About half an hour into the project, their initial attempts fall over, and there is a little squabbling as they try to figure out what has gone wrong. We break out some pencils, paper, and clipboards, and they start to create designs. Watching other groups and stealing their best ideas is encouraged.

After about 90 minutes, I force them to take a break and eat snacks amid the debris that fills the room. I lead a small discussion and elicit some general suggestions about what has and has not worked. I then explain that we have a time limit, and they will need to finish in the next hour. A few look worried. We clean up the snack quickly. Decisions are made, paper towers start to rise.

Near the end of the hour, I retrieve my camera from the closet and take pictures of each group in front of its creation—part sculpture, part architecture. Although some look less sturdy than others, the designs are all successful, although none of them are the same. One is a long, low prism that I have to lie down and squiggle to enter. Another is a cube with a roof and looks like a child's drawing of a house. The third group has managed a tall, thin teepee that they have decorated with a small flag. The last is more of a rectangle, supported on all sides with tripods. I have to sit and duck my head, but, still, I fit. The pictures, when they are developed, will show a lot of smiling, proud faces.

At lunch we vote as a class to forestall demolition in favor of eating on the floor. Several of the creations will fall over of their own accord before we finish. I sit in my armchair, at the front of the room, and there is a moment when everything just feels right. I remember reading somewhere in a description of the medieval view of the world that every person has a place in the structure of the universe. Until they find that niche, they agitate, but once their proper position is located, they calm, become still, and are happy. At this time, in this wingback chair in a preposterously decorated room where 19 sixth graders sit beside large, flimsy paper structures on a floor covered in tape and newspaper remnants, I have that brief sense that this is my proper place.

The Contents of My Backpack

It is an unassuming looking L. L. Bean daypack with two large compartments in back, a smaller forward compartment, and a little zippered pocket in the very front. The color is a shiny but somewhat muted metallic blue. My last name is scrawled in faded blue marker on the silver reflective stripe that runs across the pack's face. Fully loaded, it weighs a good 20 pounds. I wear it in the ultimate uncool fashion, high on my back and with the belt firmly cinched around my waist.

I have spent over half of my career as a migrant teacher, working in other people's rooms rather than having a space of my own. My backpack has become my mobile classroom. As a teacher, I carry all sorts of things with me to work: my hopes, my knowledge, my prejudices, and all of the emotional baggage of my own experience. And it also helps me to drag around a large pack full of assorted junk.

My inspirational "welcome to teaching math" talk was not going well. Four faces looked back at me—three women, one man, all in their early 20s. They appeared to be no more confident in their grasp of the subject matter than they had been before my presentation, possibly less so. For these teaching interns this would be their first real taste of teaching on their own. At least two of the four have confessed to being math phobic. All of them had requested English for their first assignment.

I placed my backpack on the table. After the presentation of the formal agenda and my carefully prepared overhead transparencies, the backpack looked almost dramatic.

"OK," I told the interns, "much of what we have been talking about has been theoretical. I believe in theory— you have to know why you are doing what you are doing. But the truth is that nothing theoretical is going to be all that helpful to you right now. You need some tricks."

I had their attention again. All four stared at the backpack as if they were expecting it to get up and do a little dance. It just sat there, heavy and solid, listing slightly to one side.

"These are my tricks; you will need to develop your own. But the first rule of survival as a teacher is to learn to be a good thief. Steal whatever you need from wherever you can get it. Most of what I have here I have stolen and adapted from other teachers, things I've read, workshops, and advice from strangers on the street. If any of these things look like they might work for you, use them.

Teaching is about heart and soul and knowledge and skill, but when it comes down to it, none of that matters unless you master the physics of the classroom. You have to control time, space, and stuff. These three things will make or break you, and the choices you make about how to deal with them will determine what kind of a classroom you will have. There is no magic to controlling time, space, and stuff, but there are a lot of little things you can do that make a world of difference. Tricks. It helps to have a bag of tricks.

> You have to control time, space, and stuff. These three things will make or break you.

This one, this monstrosity of future back problems, is mine."

Outside Front Pocket

Item 1: a kitchen timer. Possibly the most effective classroom management tool that I use. Much of teaching involves getting students to do what you want them to do within certain time restrictions. If you let them, students will spend the entire class period looking for their homework.

The timer changes everything. My current timer is of a simple, circular design in a schoolbus yellow, it has a magnet on the back so that I can stick it on the chalkboard (most chalkboards are magnetized), and it dangles from a string so that I can hang it coach-style around my neck. I used to have one that looked like a hamburger, but I dropped it once too often.

For most people, standard time units like five minutes, half an hour, and 15 minutes are meaningless. The timer gives these units meaning. I tend to allot odd amounts of time for tasks because they sound more precise, and people seem more aware of the interval. I give 17 minutes for most cooperative problem-solving activities, 6 minutes works well for a quick-write prompt, and one-minute stretch breaks work wonders.

When I ask a question, I give my students two minutes to work out the answer, including conferring with their neighbors. In most classrooms, a teacher asks a question and expects someone to know the answer right away. This limits the kinds of questions these teachers can ask. It makes class feel like hosting "Jeopardy." Two minutes is enough time to change that dynamic.

When the buzzer goes off, I decide whether we need more time. The actual time we spend on something isn't really that important; I don't plan my lessons to the minute. What the timer provides is a sense of urgency, a little more focus. I start every class by saying "We have a lot to do today." We always do, of course. Why else would we be here?

Item 2: a flat flashlight. I was a Boy Scout. Enough said.

Small Front Compartment

Item 1: pencils and pens. I collect them off the floor at the end of class. Sometimes I buy a box if I see them cheap. Most of my pens are giveaways from politicians, dry cleaners, and real estate agents. They aren't fine writing instruments, but I will lose most of them anyway.

Yes, students should be prepared for class. Yes, they should be responsible for their supplies. In a perfect world you could hand out the trusty No. 2 pencils on day one and expect students to keep them in neat little pencil boxes, sharpening them until they disappear into their barely used erasers.

There are only so many things I can worry about. In my mind, the greater lessons about the responsibilities of pen and pencil ownership don't rank up there with everything else I'm trying to teach. I lose pens all the time. I try very hard not to ask students to do things I'm not willing to do—such as keep track of a cheap pencil. If someone needs something to write with, give him or her something to write with. If you are anal, get some pencils with your name printed on them and ask for them back.

Item 2: chalk, dry erase markers, and a few Sharpies. One of the joys of borrowing space is that you can never be sure whether what you need will be there. Little things like a garbage can, or a window shade, or heat in the winter are often missing. You can't bring a furnace with you to class, but you can carry your own chalk. If you plan to write on the board, lack of chalk is a major disruption.

Sharpie markers are pure gold. They write better and last longer than regular magic markers. Other teachers always want to borrow them. Often, you must threaten bodily harm to get them back.

Item 3: playing cards (several decks in various states of disrepair) and a two-headed coin. It all comes back to physics—time, space, and stuff. No matter how knowledgeable, witty, or entertaining you are, if you don't control these three elements, you will not create an environment conducive to learning. On the other hand, a little forethought about your class routines will make all sorts of things possible. I use my yellow kitchen timer to control time. I use my cards to control space.

The first thing I do when I enter a classroom is rearrange the space.

The first thing I do when I enter a classroom is rearrange the space. I adapt it to whatever we will be doing that day. I put the chairs together if we will be working in groups or make a circle for discussions (a big semicircle if we will be using the board or some other visual). Worse case scenario, we sit on the floor.

I have different cards for different purposes. One set is simply the remnant of a standard deck, one card for each student and a few extras for wild cards. If possible, I try to separate the students in my classes by suit. I write the name of each student in the class on a card with my trusty Sharpie.

After I arrange the room, I deal out a card to each desk so that the students know where to sit. Occasionally, I assign partners or groups ahead of time, but mostly I do it by random shuffle. I get fewer complaints that way. I think it feels less forced if cosmic rather than teacher caprice is to blame.

My second deck is mostly face cards. I have cut the cards in half with craft scissors so that they have a scalloped middle. Very tasteful. These are movement cards, useful when we need to assign partners for an activity during class or when I'm subbing and don't have cards with names on them. I count out enough sets for the class, mix well, and pass them out. Matching the two halves creates teams of two, three of a kind works well for triplets; flushes or straights can produce larger teams.

My insistence on random pairing is philosophical. I believe that students should be able to work together and should have the opportunity to work with all their classmates. The cards simply reinforce this point.

I also use the cards to call on students in class. When I ask a question or require a volunteer, I pull a card. No amount of avoiding eye contact or sitting on hands saves anyone. Everyone has to participate. They begin to appreciate the science of probability. I know that without the cards, I tend to call on some students more than others, even when I am making an effort to include everyone in a discussion. I call on males more often than females, more active students than quiet ones. My marked-up decks remove me from the equation.

When I don't want to be fair, I use my two-headed quarter. I make a number of decisions using this coin, and, after the first time, the students recognize it right off. It is important for students to learn that sometimes there aren't options.

Large Front Pocket

Item 1: a ruler. Mine has "Mr. Goldman" written on the back of it and is good and solid. I can't remember where I stole it from.

Item 2: an inbox (actually the folded up lid of a box of file folders). On the side, I have written the word "in." Box tops don't fold and unfold well, so by mid-semester it becomes more of an on-box. We move from time and space to stuff. I have so much respect for those teachers who have proper folders for everything and can convince their students to keep perfect notebooks. Organization is always a struggle for me. I do my best to establish some classroom routines. One of my goals is to reduce the amount of time we spend doing "maintenance"— collecting and checking homework, writing down assignments, distributing handouts, listening to excuses.

As soon as the room is set, I place the inbox on an empty desk, set the timer, and write the homework on the board. From day one, I ask them to do the same things: find their desks, put the homework due in the inbox, and write down the new assignment. I almost always collect all of the homework each time, even if all I do with it is hand it back to them for use later in class, just to establish the routine. I figure four minutes is enough time to spend on these activities. It feels like a drill, and it isn't the most relaxed start, but we also don't spend the entire class looking for a homework assignment. If it isn't in the box before the buzzer goes off, it's late.

If this sounds harsh, you haven't spent enough time watching middle schoolers look for their homework. They will flip through their notebooks, since they rarely write in them sequentially. Then, swearing that they know they packed it, they will thumb through each of their folders two or three times, and then, just to be sure, they will empty out the accumulated garbage from the bottom of their backpacks. I don't like to have to guess whether this is a complicated ruse or an actual case of disorganization. Part of every homework assignment includes turning it in. It isn't complete unless I have it in my inbox.

True story: I used to teach a two-year math sequence for grades 5 and 6. Once a student and I were going through his backpack looking for a sixth grade assignment, and we found several that he had failed to hand in the previous year. He looked at me and said, with a straight face, "Is it too late to turn these in now?"

Almost as frequently as I'm told that it has to be somewhere in this backpack, I am told that they already gave me the assignment. In my classroom, the rule is that you may not hand me anything. I have a bad tendency to put things down where they don't belong. Everything has to go into the inbox. I then pack it in my bag. If the assignment was placed in the box, it will still be in the box when I look for it. When I grade assignments, I grade what's in the box. It is there, or it isn't.

Large Back Pocket

Item 1: scrap paper (some of it cut in halves).
I hate wasting paper. I tend to rummage near photocopy machines and use the backs of whatever someone has left there. Most of the time we don't need nice, clean paper for what we are doing.

Item 2: office supply kit. One stapler, extra staples, paper clips, the Oxford Set of Mathematical Instruments (complete and accurate and packed in a cute little metal box), sticky notes in various sizes, a calculator, washable colored markers in several colors—including sandy brown I use for grading papers—cellophane tape, a small roll of string, some non-scrap paper, a pad of graph paper, and a thick eraser. I also carry a stapleless stapler that sort of clips the papers together by punching a hole through them. It isn't really necessary, but my stapler jams a lot, and it's just one of those cool little gadgets I couldn't resist.

In a small plastic bag I keep two self-inking stamps—a smiley face and one that says "checked" in two colors. Students won't work for grades, but they will do almost anything to have their paper stamped with a smiley face. Go figure.

Item 3: Books. Don Rubin's *Brain Storms*, Click and Clack's *A Haircut in Horse Town and Other Great Car Talk Puzzlers*, Will Shortz's *The Puzzlemaster Presents*, and *Games Magazine: The Book of Sense and Nonsense Puzzles.* The short story of my teaching career has been the search for ways to reach all my students. There are some very good teachers who believe strongly that they lay it out there, and it is up to their pupils to take or not, but that isn't me. I know I can't force someone to learn, but isn't that, in some ways, my job? Maybe force isn't the right word. Entice? Convince? Inspire?

I still talk too much in class, but at least I'm no longer under the illusion that the students listen.

When I first started teaching, I talked a lot. I told students what I wanted them to know. When that didn't work, I tried to improve the presentation—more visuals, better visuals, notes to go with the visuals. I still do these things when I talk, and I still talk too much in class, but at least I'm no longer under the illusion that the students listen.

So, the timer goes off, all of the homework is in the inbox, all of the students are in their proper seats, and we are finally ready to start class. I figure that I can, at most, accomplish three things in a 45-minute period.

All my lesson plans look pretty much the same:

1. Warm-up—usually a mental math exercise, but sometimes something small, such as reviewing a particular homework question that everyone missed.

2. An activity—preferably one that is more like a project.

3. Wrap-up—the truth is that I almost never leave time for an organized closer. Often, I just ask the students what they learned from doing the activity.

If I have done a good job preparing, the activity part should run itself. Whenever possible, I avoid oral instructions altogether and pass out written directions with the materials. There are times when I find myself standing at the front of the room watching my students work, unsure about what I should be doing. I try not to hover. If I'm really bored, I'll dig out my two-headed coin and practice my French drop.

Most days, however, there is enough for me to do— answering questions about my poorly written instructions, redirecting unfocused students, offering a little extra help. In addition to involving students much more actively in the lesson, the advantage of the emphasis on small projects is that it allows students, alone or as part of a team, to work at their pace. The disadvantage is that it allows students, alone or as part of a team, to work at their own pace.

When I create a project, I try to picture a large room full of beautifully wrapped presents. At a minimum, it is the job of every student to retrieve and open one gift. Usually it is a small thing, one objective that no one should finish the project without accomplishing. I set my sights low for this goal: exposure to a new idea, practice with numbers, the definition of one key term. If it is a well-conceived activity, the room contains many more presents to open, from simple extensions to self-guided explorations. At whatever pace the students work, there should always be something more to do—preferably, something relevant, productive, and yet interesting enough so that it doesn't feel like punishment.

It is not always possible to create a lesson that works on so many levels. Sometimes when the activity is a little more shallow, like correcting our notebooks, some students finish early, while others need more time and guidance. If I am organized, I have a set of challenge activities taped to note cards. If not, I have my puzzle books. The challenges in these books call for problem solving, logic, spatial sense—a host of skills students need to practice. The puzzles are never strictly required (although there is always a section of my students' portfolios dedicated to "ways I have gone beyond the course requirements"), and most students like them.

I don't believe in wasting time. Learning is not a process with an endpoint. As long as we have ticks on the timer, I have at least one more activity we can do hidden somewhere in the depths of my backpack.

Open the zippers, shake the backpack, and out comes a pile of debris: books and office supplies, paper, playing cards, and kitchen implements. A flashlight. Some string. These are not the tools I think about when I think about teaching. They are the incidentals, just stuff. Nothing in the bag helps a student read more deeply, write more clearly, or balance an equation. I don't even have a good map in the bag (note to self: find and pack small map). Yet this load of junk I drag around with me contains the props I need to create the classroom—to manipulate the time, space, and stuff necessary to transform ordinary rooms into arenas for ideas.

My backpack, still fully loaded, now sits in the back of my closet. When I left teaching to become a full-time parent, I cleaned out my files, ditched my old grade books and moved most of my educational library to the basement. I sat for a while, trying to figure out what to do with all the paraphernalia in my pack. Some of it could have been tossed, reshelved, mixed in with my other belongings. Part of me still isn't ready to dismantle it. I can't imagine any scenario in which I would need to grab it and rush off to a classroom—an emergency math lesson or something—but the backpack is a piece of who I am. And it still feels right to keep it ready. It might be years before I need it, assuming I ever do, but it is comforting to know that all of my stuff is still packed away, everything together, waiting—part memento, part storage for some of what I've learned thus far. It is the stuff of teaching—my autobiography in a bag.

Why I Show Up

Oren is late. This is not an unusual event. Oren has been late every day this year, and, according to school legend, he hasn't shown up on time for any event after his initial kindergarten interview.

Oren's stepfather comes in to apologize. Oren's mother, he explains, just can't seem to get him out of the house in the morning. I'm not sure why he thinks this is a valid excuse. He also wants to check in with me about how Oren is doing. It does no good to explain that I am trying to get my class started, that they are all sitting in there waiting for me. At this point in the morning, armed only with my one cup of coffee, I can't think of a good way to make this man understand that, even though they have been helping with Oren's homework, they are still, as a family, failing math.

I suggest that maybe we set up another family meeting, and he eventually goes off to work. I wonder what job he has that lets him show up late every day.

No one in the class seems to have a pencil. The pencil jar is empty, and my back-up supply in the closet has been exhausted. Students are scrounging around the floor, checking under the radiator, emptying out their backpacks. Aaron found a splintered remnant by the bookshelf and is taping it together with way too much cellophane tape. Rachel is busy explaining to anyone who will listen how she has been using the same pencil for most of the semester and that it is still a good inch-and-a-half long and capped with a generous remnant of pink eraser. Naomi opens her pencil box and reluctantly doles out the four pencils inside, each accompanied with the dire warning that these are her *special* pencils that she brought from home and that she wants them back without teeth marks.

This is not how I imagined this lesson beginning. Nowhere in my planning had I allowed for a major pencil crisis.

Eventually everyone has some form of a writing implement. Nicholas has a stub so small that it is nearly invisible behind his thick fingers. Reggie is using a ballpoint pen that leaves large blotches on everything he writes. A few students are using some of the darker shades of the art pencils, but we have managed to avoid having to use the magic markers, and no one has to share. The day officially begins.

I hand out a worksheet on fractions that I had hoped would provide a serene entry to our school day. I place one copy in each student's hand, afraid that the process of passing the stack around might unleash further chaos. Everyone settles into reading the instructions, and there is a brief moment of quiet. I check the clock. We have 10 minutes before they need to go to science.

....

Today must be Zipper Day. I hadn't noticed it until almost recess, but that must be the theme. Almost everything Naomi, Jennifer, and Rachel are wearing has at least one zipper, including each of Jennifer's shoes.

Zipper Day is among the more subtle theme days that this threesome has celebrated this year. One day in September, without warning, it was Princess Day, and they wore flowing nightgowns and pointy cone headpieces. Some days have been devoted to particular colors, others to styles of jewelry, and at least one to an animal theme. That was easier to spot because Jennifer drew long black whiskers on her face.

What amazes me most is not that I have six graders who come to school in costume. That is odd, but not that odd. The most incredible thing about these theme days is how little they seem to interrupt class. Rachel kept talking into her "communicator" on Star Trek Day, reporting all of our activities to the Enterprise, but with that exception, all three girls manage to go about their school day as if their outrageous get-ups are perfectly normal. I learned early on that the appropriate adult response was to pretend I didn't notice that three of my students had their clothes on backwards or were dressed like hippies with magic marker peace signs on their cheeks.

....

Nicholas has a question. If I hesitate to call on him, it is only because I need to gauge how much disruption I think the class can handle. He is holding his hand up, waving it slowly from side to side. Something between a wave and a drowning man's call for help.

Nicholas always has a question. It is rarely relevant. He will ask me about string theory during English and interrupt a math lesson with his thoughts on state politics. If I let him go on long enough he will detail the line of thought that led him from my discussion of the Middle Ages to his question about the Aztec calendar, but I rarely let him go on that long.

"Is this a question or a comment?"

He thinks for a moment. "A question."

"Is it at all relevant to what we are discussing?"

"Sort of," he answers. I know that "sort of" means not at all, but I give in. Jerome groans and lays his head on his desk even before Nicholas has a chance to speak. Not everyone appreciates Nicholas's questions.

Nicholas is a little chubby, and his parents have let him dye part of his brown hair blue. When he was in kindergarten he would come to school in full costume everyday—a fireman, or a cowboy, or a businessman with a coat and tie. Now he mostly wears sweat pants and t-shirts. He does not participate in the Jennifer, Rachel, and Naomi theme days, although I suspect he might want to. His current passion is the electric guitar, and he and James were recently caught sitting on Charles Street playing the blues, guitar cases open for donations.

"If the Romans had aqueducts and running water, why did people in eighteenth century Paris still throw their...," he pauses to search for a school-appropriate word. I hold my breath and hope he finds one.

"...crap out the window into the street."

A plumbing question, and not a simplistic one. I suspect the answer has to do with the way technical information is lost and refound as civilizations rise and fall, but the truth is that I don't know how to answer this question with more than some suppositions and generalizations.

"I'm not really sure, Nicholas. What do you think?"

"I think maybe that you need hills to make aqueducts work, and maybe Paris doesn't have hills."

Even when I used to be a Latin teacher, I never found the mechanics of aqueducts interesting, so, although I know they use gravity, I'm not sure how much of a slope is required and how much is generated artificially by the way the structures are constructed. I suggest to Nicholas that we consult Ms. Demos, our librarian, who I am convinced can find the answer to any question, and try to refocus the discussion on the current topic: predicates.

....

Oren and Will are in trouble again. They both have that adolescent puppy look that some boys develop at this age when their bodies are growing faster than their coordination. Neither can sit in their seats for any length of time without spilling out one direction or the other. Their arms flail; their heads roll about their shoulders. I suspect both will be taller than me by the end of the year, but they still look like such little kids. The Spanish teacher has both of them sitting out in the hall as I return for lunch.

"We didn't do anything," Oren tells me before I have a chance to ask.

"What is Señora Martin going to tell me when I ask her?"

This is actually a mean question because it requires them to tell the other side of the story first. But it also spares me from having to tell Oren that I don't believe him.

"She'll say we were playing around and not listening," Oren chooses to go generic.

"I was listening, or trying to listen, but Oren kept making me laugh." Will is the more earnest of the two and always sells Oren out. I wonder how they stay friends. I sit down next to them.

"It doesn't seem to be asking too much for you to pay attention in class. What can you guys do to keep this from happening?"

"We probably shouldn't sit together," Will says, sighing. Standard answer.

"Good start."

"Or look at each other during class," Oren offers.

I wait; there has to be more.

"We could apologize to Señora Martin?" Will asks. I'm not sure why this is a question, but I nod.

"You know, if this continues, I'm going to have to sit in on all the Spanish classes again."

Their eyes get big. Not that!

"Can I trust you to keep it together better than today?"

They both nod.

I figure this talk will last about two weeks,

> I've noticed that, with each passing year, I find it easier and easier to play the heavy.

enough to get us to winter break. What I can't figure out is why it should even last that long. I've noticed that, with each passing year, I find it easier and easier to play the heavy. Once I had a student tell me that I wasn't mean enough. Oren and Will would find that hard to believe.

....

Alice doesn't have lunch, again. We are a brown bag school—no cafeteria, not even a soda machine. Everybody brings a lunch, except Alice. Her family is one of the wealthiest in the school. Her father, an inventor and entrepreneur, holds several important patents, and her mother is an artist. As a family, they have creativity to spare but lack some essential organizational skills. Like an ability to get their children to school with reasonable lunches.

Often Alice improvises. Bread and a small block of cheese. Some sort of leftovers. Once, a jar of capers. More frequently, she mooches off of Emma whose mother seems to pack an enormous variety of foods. Emma often carries her lunch in a grocery sack. They make a good pair.

I send Alice upstairs to the teachers' lounge where I keep a loaf of bread in the freezer and a jar of peanut butter in the fridge. I label both as property of the sixth grade, but people seem to appropriate my supplies anyway. I wouldn't mind if they would also occasionally replace them. Or at least let me know when they are used up.

Alice comes back with plain, dry toast. She doesn't like peanut butter. Emma hands her an apple. I spend the rest of the period trying to enforce the "no maggot" rule. Several weeks ago I outlawed any discussion of maggots at the lunch table. In theory, all talking at lunch was already limited to polite conversation, but after Nicholas discovered that Jennifer shuddered whenever she heard the word "maggot," it became necessary to specify the boundaries of appropriate lunch topics. Nevertheless, Nicholas seems to find ways of working maggots into a variety of conversational subjects. My job, as I see it, is to provide enough resistance so that he at least has to be creative about it.

....

Oren writes a poem, just in time for our class's literary magazine deadline. Oren had been the only student without an entry. Rachel has submitted at least six, including two about the Holocaust and one obscure one, which might be about death or perhaps about being afraid of the dark—it is a little hard to tell. Oren has been feeling the pressure.

He sits hunched over the computer keyboard, a position he has maintained for most of the last hour. There is something in Oren's build and face that makes me think he might play hockey when he gets to high school, or maybe football. He is large for his age, slightly chunky but solid. His face is heavily freckled, and he flushes easily. He tends to talk in phrases rather than sentences.

"How's it going Oren?"

"Go'in."

"Can I look at it?"

Oren leans back in his chair and lets me look at the screen. He smiles across the room at Will, who is sitting on the rug next to the bookcase on the thin premise that he is reading. Will pretends to ignore Oren to avoid getting himself into trouble but ends up giggling. I send him back to his desk.

Oren's poem is about three lines long. The first line is:

Happy O! Happy O! Happy OOOOOOOOO!!!!!
At least he's happy.

And there is, at least, something here on paper we can work with, although it is a bit of a challenge to have a serious discussion about a poem proceeding from a simple "Happy O!" I remark on the exuberance of the expression, and we toy with the remaining lines, drawing out what might make an O happy and how best to express that idea. I have some concern about the pronunciation of "OOOOOOOOO!!!!" but with a little prodding Oren is able to add another two lines. The result is almost startling. If I hadn't been witness to the process, I might have chosen it as one of the most original, creative, and musical poems the class has produced. Oren isn't sure what it means, and he cannot explain any of the choices he made. Can someone write a great poem mostly by accident?

....

There is always a price of exit. Everyone, except Reggie, is packed up and sitting in his or her chair, more or less quietly. "More or less quietly" is my new euphemism for not screaming.

Like most of the class, rather than trying to figure out what he really needs, he just takes everything out of his small locker and dumps it into his backpack.

I no longer wait for Reggie. I cannot fathom why it takes him so long to pack up his things at the end of the day.

He isn't particularly neat about it; there is nothing in his approach that looks systematic. Like most of the class, rather than trying to figure out what he really needs, he just takes everything out of his small locker and dumps it into his backpack. He isn't socializing and doesn't appear distracted. If anything, he looks unusually focused. At most, this should be a two-minute operation.

All the class jobs are complete. The board has been erased. The larger pieces of floor debris have been picked up. The supplies have been returned to the supply shelf. The pencil jar has two pencils in it: the one Aaron taped together earlier today and one of Naomi's. A donation. Someone must have chewed on it. I will have to remember to go buy some more.

The price of exit is always some piece of information. It has been a long day, so I set the bar low. All I want is an adverb from each of them. No repeats.
Hands go up.

"Quickly," says Naomi, almost running to line up at the door.
"Slowly," offers Jerome. Involuntarily I check to see if Reggie has made any progress.
"Now?" asks Nicholas, when I call on him. I nod. "Now," he pronounces and lines up at the door. I should give extra credit for clever word play.

Most of the others stick to adverbs ending in "ly." Will offers "fastly" and has to try again. Rachel, second-to-last, gives a convincing performance of "dejectedly" as she slumps toward the door.

Reggie is finally ready. Since he hasn't been listening, his first few suggestions are all repeats. The line grows frustrated.

"What time is it Reggie?" I ask.

"3:15."

"And that makes us…"

"Late."

"Great adverb. Let's go." I nod to Naomi at the front of the line, and she leads the class up the stairs.

....

After Jennifer, who is always the last to be picked up, finally climbs into her car, I go to the teachers' room to check my voice mail. There are two new messages. The first is from Reggie's dad, who wants me to tell Reggie to take the bus home. Reggie left with his regular carpool half an hour ago. The second is from Lauren's mother following up on the two-page note she sent in with her daughter today. Lauren's mother writes very nice notes—a little on the chatty side, but always polite. She was hoping to talk to me between 2 and 3 o'clock. That would have been English class. I'll call her tonight.

I return to my classroom. It is a mess. Every surface seems to have something left on it. There is Reggie's baseball hat. Nicholas's homework folder is lying on the floor. There is a sock next to the computer keyboard. A sock? How did I miss someone taking off a sock?

More disturbingly, a lot of the mess is mine. Not the sock, however. Before the school year began, I gave up my desk in the interest of having more space, but that has left me with nowhere to put my stuff. There are stacks of paper lying on the windowsill, on the computer table, on a chair in the back of the room, and in small piles in front of the blackboard. My coffee cup is perched on the filing cabinet. My lunchbox is sitting on one of the student tables near the back of the classroom. It must have been there all afternoon. They must have just worked around it.

I am too tired to do anymore today. I throw my notebook and some stacks of paper into my backpack and retrieve my lunch box. I will have some work to do tonight. And I need to call Lauren's mother. I stop and survey the wreck of my classroom. If I get in early, I can get it back in shape before the students show up in the morning.

This is how I spend my days. It isn't exactly running into burning buildings and rescuing babies. I am not orchestrating successful business mergers or performing heart surgery. It isn't even really about curriculum or learning targets or fractions. Well, it's a little bit about fractions. Often it is about pencils and giggling in class and irrelevant questions and discussing maggots at lunch. Piece by piece it never feels like much. And yet, it feels like something. Not at the end of every day. There are days that feel totally pointless. But not often. It is a little like staring at a Seurat painting. The picture isn't in any particular dot or even any cluster of dots. But the dots matter.

On my walk home, I pass Alice who is stomping on chestnuts in the public garden. The sidewalk is covered with broken outer husks and well-stomped brown kernels. She lives only a few blocks from the school but clearly hasn't made it home yet. She looks up at me suspiciously, weighing the possibility that this activity might somehow get her into trouble. I smile and wish her a pleasant afternoon. The words sound archaic, but they are heartfelt. It is a beautiful fall day, and this is a beautiful space for jumping up and down on chestnuts.

Alice's response is a look somewhere between quizzical and frowning, but she mutters a "bye" and follows it with a half-wave. I leave her to her chestnut stomping and walk past my favorite monument, the one celebrating the discovery that ether can be used as anesthesia. This particular fountain has not been operational for years, and the white stone is streaked and graying, but something about the whole idea of an ether monument amuses me.

"Pencils," I think to myself. "I need to buy some more pencils." I pass behind the statue of George Washington astride his horse, wend my way to the Arlington Street exit, and head home.

Four Square and the Politics of Sixth Grade Lunch

One of the first things I do when I enter the classroom is rearrange the furniture. Before we can begin, we have to define our space. I do my best to make everyone feel like they have a place. We work in partners a lot, but no one ever chooses with whom they work. Seats are chosen randomly (or almost randomly) at the beginning of each class. No one ever is relegated to a certain spot; there are no cool rows. Despite my best efforts, there are two events that I find I can't control. One is walking in line. Assigning partners for walking in line turns out to be counterproductive, because unless you march everyone military style, kids simply ignore unwanted partners and bunch together with their friends. I try to avoid having students walk in lines. The other is lunch. It is hard to avoid having students eat lunch. In the less regulated environment of lunchtime—and there must be some times during the day when we relax a bit—it is possible to talk over and around anyone in the way. It is a classic lead-a-horse-to-water scenario. I can force them to sit next to one another, but I can't make it a pleasant dining experience.

For the last several years, I have become fascinated with lunch. I have spent my teaching career almost entirely within small schools. Small schools rarely have cafeterias, so lunch frequently has taken place in my classroom. As a consequence, I have become more comfortable with both rodents and insects. We put the books away, clear the desks, pull out the brown bags. I carry the same Sesame Street lunch box I used to carry down Michigan Avenue in my brief stint in a 9-to-5 job. There it was a small act of rebellion. Here, it's just another strange thing Mr.Goldman does.

....

Every class has its own unique lunch dynamic. In my first school, my room was furnished with combo desk chairs, you know, the kind with a plastic chair with the desk attached. They were very easy to rearrange, and I let the students move them around however they wanted during lunch. It was fascinating to watch the patterns. You could tell a lot about a class by the arrangement of chairs. My first eighth-grade homeroom sat in two loosely organized groups: one for boys, one for girls. As noticing turned into flirting and flirting became "dating," the edges of the clusters began to gravitate toward one another. Location began to become a small map of differential maturity, with the boys who wanted nothing to do with girls on the outskirts on one side, the interactants in the middle, and the girls who weren't sure about boys on the far side.

The next year's class was ruled by four dominant girls who consciously and effectively set the social hierarchy. Instead of two separate clusters, this was a spiral galaxy slowly unwinding from the center desks of the committee of four. The closer to the center, the closer to power and favor, with the far-flung stars condemned to the outer reaches of the universe, the area near—God forbid—my desk. My last eighth grade homeroom was less socially rigid and tended to sit in little clumps—three or four students to a clump, with some variation week to week. The non-clumped students tended to sit wherever the chairs happened to have been left from the last class, which could be virtually anywhere. Lunch became a study in fractals—constantly changing, beautifully complex patterns.

Lunch became a study in fractals-constantly changing, beautifully complex patterns.

Lunch this way was OK, but something about it irked me. I guess I spent too much time wondering where I would have been allowed to sit. Although each class had its own arrangement, in all three scenarios there were kids that could claim the most valuable real estate, and kids that couldn't.

A few years and two jobs later, I found myself back at a school without a cafeteria. This time, I had a sixth grade homeroom, and this time I was determined to make lunch a better social experience. I had been allowed to order new furniture, and I asked for trapezoidal tables instead of desks. There are several advantages to trapezoids. Alone they sit two comfortably, three if they need to work as a committee. Put two trapezoids together, and six can sit around the resulting hexagon. Six of the trapezoids can be lined up to make one long conference table around which we can comfortably seat almost the whole class. Armed with my trapezoids, we were going to eat lunch together as one big, happy family. We were going to be saved by geometry. Everyone would have a place at this table.

And some years it worked, more or less. The students grumbled a little as I had them rearrange the room for lunch, but it provided a transition. I did not assign seats, but I didn't allow saving seats either. Most of the time everyone got to sit near someone he or she wanted to sit with, and there were surprisingly few fights. In nearly every class, most of the students eventually chose regular seats, which they sat in every day. If someone wasn't in his or her regular seat, it was usually a good barometer that something was happening that would soon need my attention.

And then came the year I had Michael in my class. Michael was new to the school. To adults he came across as a mostly likeable, intelligent young man, but it was clear he lacked an ability to recognize and interpret social cues. On his first day, unprompted, he announced that he could beat anyone in any video game and that he was an amazing basketball player. He repeated these claims at least three times. He frequently told me that he had already learned whatever it was I was trying to teach

him, although he couldn't ever quite remember just how
it went when he was called on. He often interrupted
conversations between other students and blurted out
inappropriate things. He was impossible to pair up in line,
and he could not find a place at the class table.

In that class there were 19 students, one teacher, and
an intern who ate lunch with us. By the second or third
week when all the students had found their "regular"
seats, the class had split itself by gender—10 girls on
the right side of the table, 8 boys on the left. In most of
the classes, boys had tended to sit with boys and girls
with girls, but this was the first class to split the table
cleanly into a boys' side and a girls' side. There should
have been more than enough room for Michael on the
boys' side—the girls managed to squeeze all 10 in. But to
find a place, Michael would have to break into the line at
some point. Nothing he tried worked. He would bring his
chair and try to squeeze it in between people, only to be
effectively squeezed back out so that he became a second
row. If he ran to the table and claimed a spot, he would
find the neighbors on either side turned away so that he
was an island of space between two tighter clumps of
conversation. For a while, Michael became increasingly
slow about retrieving his lunch, would disappear to the
bathroom for up to half the period, complain that there
were no places left, and try to sit by himself away from
the table.

But it wasn't just Michael. Even for kids who were not
physically excluded, lunch seemed more tense. It was as
if everyone, that is everyone except for Michael, had been

assigned a seat number by some power I couldn't see. This device, my family table, became the battleground of a subtle but powerful caste system enforced through rather sophisticated social interplay.

What was going on? As I watched it unfold, it all seemed strangely familiar. And then I realized where I had seen these patterns before. Recess. Not all of recess, but a particular game called four square.

In theory, the game of four square is pretty simple. A 4'x 4' box is drawn, or, in most schools painted, on the pavement. The box is divided into four equal quadrants, called squares. One player stands in each square. The person in Square 1 gets to serve, which means that player bounces the ball in his or her own square and then taps it so that it lands in one of the other three squares. If the ball lands in your square, you have to tap it into someone else's square. If it bounces twice in your square, or if you hit it out of bounds, then you are out. This is how four square might be played if it were regulated by adults. But unlike almost all other recess sports, four square remains almost entirely a kid's game and still retains kid rules. In pickup football and basketball games, a player can refer to the official (the "adult") rules for the authority they need to sustain a claim of injustice. No such authority exists for four square. When an adult intervenes, as I frequently tried to do when I first started monitoring recess, the kids quickly lose interest and find other games. But left alone, the same group of students can play four square every recess for years. They'll play it in the rain, clear off the snow from the court, endure freezing weather for it.

I've watched students play it with deflated balls. What about this game inspires such devotion? Students play it because they understand, long before adults get it, that four square is not a sport. Four square is a ruthless game of politics.

Each quadrant has a number. A new player always enters at Square 4. If a player in one of the other squares is eliminated, the players in the lower squares are promoted in order: 4 to 3: 3 to 2; 2 to 1. Square 1 is the prime objective. In addition to the status of achieving the top spot, the player in Square 1 has several distinct advantages. First, he or she serves. Inexperienced players are usually knocked out before a rally is even begun and are easy targets for the server. Most important, however, is that the player in Square 1 gets to make the rules.

Students play it because they understand, long before adults get it, that four square is not a sport. Four square is a ruthless game of politics.

Layout of a four square court:

1	2
4	3

Four square rules differ from school to school and range from the simple to the bizarre. The server can declare no slamming—purposefully accelerating the ball to an unmanageable speed. The server can call double bounces, baby taps, or even allow people to catch the ball. A call of "bubbles" allows the players to juggle the ball with little taps so that they can better position themselves to make a slam (assuming slams are allowed). There are variations such as "graveyard," which I never quite understood but seems to involve everyone walking around and around their squares and then suddenly, on cue, racing to the middle. None of these options actually enhance the game as an athletic event. They, in fact, serve only one purpose. These rules allow the person in power to exert that power over the other players. Once you understand that the true objective of the game is to establish and maintain power, the way it is played begins to make sense. In most games I observed, Square 1 was rarely contested. This may seem ironic, since being in Square 1 is the stated goal. In practice, however, Square 1 must remain fairly stable for the political dimensions to play out. Square 1 isn't won, it is ruled. The main goal for the rest of the players is to curry favor with the ruler of Square 1, who determines who stays, who is cast out, and who is allowed to occupy which square of the hierarchy. Imagine a medieval court with nobles jostling for the position closest to the king.

Lunch in my classroom had become four square. Bear in mind that these were nice kids. They were polite. They were serious about school and truly wanted to do well. They volunteered for community service projects and read every week to the first graders. There were no real discipline issues—no punches thrown on the recess yard, no truancy, no drugs. We had one incident of vandalism when Ellen wrote on the bathroom stall that Maria was a bitch. Ellen has severe dyslexia and failed to spell any of the words correctly, so the message lacked both force and anonymity. In retrospect, I don't believe this class's lunch behavior was in any way exceptional, only a little more transparent.

Lunch in my classroom had become four square.

The six trapezoids could really only fit about 18 students, and since there were 21 of us including the teachers, we added a round table to one end. To avoid having the distinction of sitting at one of those four privileged places cause massive competition, the adults quickly established their beachhead on the extension table. Once the adults took two of those seats, the other two became the least desired places at the table. I think a diagram might be helpful.

The Lunch Table:

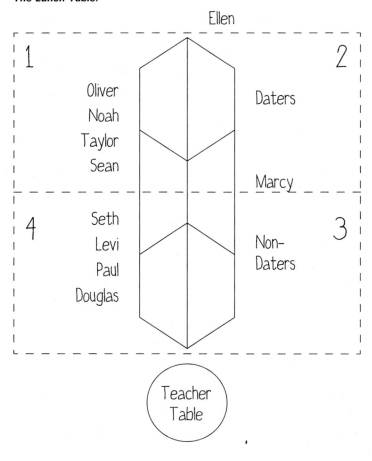

The first rule, as I had already observed, was a strict separation of the sexes. At no time, no matter how fierce the competition for seats became, was the rule willingly violated; nor did the genders ever trade sides. All other differences aside, gender remained the primary classification.

This version of four square was played in teams. Square 1, the first four seats on the left side of the table, belonged to four boys: Oliver, Noah, Taylor, and Sean—always in that order. These were the prime seats because they were as far away as you could get from the teachers without being in their direct line of sight. Sitting at the other end of a noisy table and blocked from the teacher's view by a hedge of heads was the closest thing to privacy the situation allowed. Seating desirability is inversely related to teacher proximity and control.

Oliver and Noah had been best of friends since third grade and were the self-appointed leaders of the class. Their seats waited empty for them as they wended their way slowly from the backpack hooks where we kept our lunches. The other students, even those who disliked Oliver and Noah, openly

> It is one of the paradoxes of social structure that popular is not synonymous with being well-liked.

acknowledged their popularity. It is one of the paradoxes of social structure that popular is not synonymous with being well-liked. The other two spaces in Square 1, the two immediately to the right of Oliver and Noah, remained a battleground of contention for several months. Whereas no one dared to take on the rulers of the first two seats, there were a number of boys who tried to lay claim to the second tier. There were several arguments, one pushing match, a lot of chair slamming and one or two precarious dives over the table to secure the seats first. Since saving seats was forbidden, and violence strongly discouraged, speed was the primary weapon. On more than one occasion we caught students hiding their lunches in the classroom during the period before lunch so that they could gain the advantage of not having to return to the hallway. Eventually political persuasion trumped speed, and Oliver and Noah granted the seats to two of their more loyal henchmen. The tactics weren't subtle, consisting mostly of forms of verbal abuse, but they were hard to counter since the victims were required to laugh along with the tormentors, and they eventually moved down the row. Sean and Taylor, the recipients of Oliver and Noah's largesse, never occupied their seats with the same assurance as their benefactors, but, with the exception of a week when Sean was somehow banished to the end of the table, they held their positions for the remainder of the year.

True to the game, Square 1 is the most stable and powerful spot. Whoever rules the first square has the power to determine the other three. Square two, the prime positions on the right side, belonged to whichever girls the boys in Square 1 were interested in. The boundary line between squares two and three was Marcy, who always sat somewhere in the middle of the pack and established the center point. Wherever she sat, Amy, her best friend, sat to her immediate right. Although they were always next to each other, the boundary between cliques was drawn between them. Amy and the girls to her right were the social hot set who dated Oliver, Noah, Taylor and Sean in different combinations. Marcy and the girls to her left were non-daters, although sometimes one or more would move to the right for a short romance and then back to the left when the affections shifted. Although the girls' side was not as rigid as the boys', the relative positions to the right and left of Marcy were faithfully enforced.

Marcy was the boundary line, but Square 3 developed a personality all its own. The last three spots on the girls' side belonged to Maria, Britney, and Stephanie. Britney was new to the class and was a little more worldly—a little wilder than her classmates. She befriended Maria early on. Maria had distinguished herself in fourth grade by dating a sixth grader, and her flirting remained a ripe topic of faculty concern bordering on gossip. Although Britney and Maria held a certain cache of coolness, they were not accepted by the rest of the girls. Maria and Britney adopted Stephanie, and the threesome became a self-sufficient unit. Denied the north end of the table, they staked out their own territory, the uncontested three spaces to the left of the teachers. One of the ironies of lunch was that I often ate it with Stephanie, a student who was, in other circumstances, often openly hostile toward me. I don't believe we ever had much of a conversation, but she never complained about the location. Maria and Britney each had a turn among the daters for a few weeks, but that didn't last long, and they were returned to the far end of the table.

The lowest rank in foursquare is the fourth square. The four seats in this square, the lower portion of the boys' side, were held in a fairly rigorous pecking order: Seth, Levi, Paul, and finally, Douglas. The arrangement reflected their level of social acceptance, although none were, strictly speaking, ever accepted into the upper echelons of the Oliver and Noah scene. Douglas made some valiant efforts to improve his station but eventually simply accepted that he had drawn the short straw and sat in the least desirable of the acceptable seats—the one next to me. To a man they expressed their disdain for the four boys in Square 1 and claimed to have rejected that social hierarchy, but none were willing to let the others move to positions closer to the power.

As in the recess game, the rulers of the first square effectively determined who occupied each of the other spots. Those they favored most sat closest. Sometimes Square 3 girls could be promoted to Square 2, but they occupied those chairs at the whim of the boys. Once the pecking order was set, Square 4 boys could pretty much count on remaining Square 4 boys for the year.

Every system reveals itself through its tensions. Since the girls' side of the table was organized by social clique, Ellen, the one girl without an established group of friends, quickly figured out that she couldn't claim a space along the spectrum. Since Britney and company had claimed the last three seats nearest the teacher, Ellen squeezed her chair on the corner of the far end of the table, a small outpost past the daters. Although it was clear she wasn't part of that group, she still held on to the very edge of the girls' side, and everyone else seemed content to let her stay there. The Square 1 boys completely ignored her. In terms of their social world, she simply didn't exist.

The major source of lunch tension in this system, however, was Michael. He could not figure out the rules of this game. The most logical place for Michael was beside Douglas, next to me at bottom of the pecking order. I invited him to sit there often, determined that he had to have a place at my communal table. This spot, however, proved to be unacceptable for two reasons. Although he wasn't able to navigate the system, Michael did understand the significance of the last spot, and he would do virtually anything to avoid accepting it. Although there was no obvious way his social status could have sunk lower, having to admit to himself that he belonged at the end of the table was more than he could assimilate. The second problem was that Douglas, of all the boys, *our boys* was the most openly hostile to Michael. Michael was all that stood between Douglas and the true bottom of the social hierarchy, and Douglas defended his slightly superior position with astounding vehemence. Oppression is not a caste system; each step of the ladder holds the one below it in check. I think on some not-so-conscious level, Douglas understood that the only bit of status he could gain was in successfully ostracizing Michael. The only thing worse than the last spot next to the teacher was no spot at all. Douglas made it impossible for Michael to sit next to him.

None of my attempts to intervene worked. For a while I broke up the family table and assigned seats at three separate hexagons, but it actually made it worse, bringing the nastiness to the surface as students loudly complained about who they had to sit next to. We used our class meeting time to talk about how we treat each other. We met in small groups. I called parents. In the end, those efforts simply drove most of the tension underground. It was harder to spot when I was around, but it still was there.

Most of the kids refused to see the problem. The popular kids said they just wanted to sit with their friends. Less popular kids complained about how cliquey some kids were but also claimed that they didn't want anything to do with those kids anyhow. Everything Michael said implied that he thought he was part of the "in" group. Taylor, the boy who occupied the third seat in Square 1, was the only student who said something that felt authentic, and I'm still disturbed by it. "I had to fight to be in the popular group," he told me. "It takes a lot. You

> "I had to fight to be in the popular group," he told me. "It takes a lot. You can't just sit there and want to be popular. You have to be willing to do what it takes."

can't just sit there and want to be popular. You have to be willing to do what it takes." Taylor felt he had earned his position. He was unrepentant.

The rules of four square are consistent on one point only. New players have to start at the bottom. If you want to play, you have to choose a spot within the order or stand outside the game. Eventually we returned to eating at my family table, and eventually Michael found a spot, but he never entered the game. He finally settled on the far side beside Ellen. Logically, this space should have been deemed cool. It was on the socially important end of the table, right beside Oliver. It was directly across from the teachers, but still three table lengths away. And yet, no one else ever tried to sit there, and Michael only resorted to it when he had no other choices.

The first problem with Michael's seat was that it was on the wrong side of Oliver. Social hierarchy was right-handed; the pecking order was firmly established as a line. Sitting to the left did not confer status; it signaled exclusion from the system. Michael's presence did not indicate a social connection to Oliver. In fact, Oliver and Michael talked a lot during lunch, although I suspect that Michael was the butt of many of the jokes. No one, however, confused his proximity with favor.

I think the second issue with the last seat was that it was perilously close to the girls. Unlike Ellen, Michael could not work his way into the corner because that would encroach on Oliver's territory. Instead, Michael ended up smack in the middle, directly across from the teachers and in the fuzzy no-man's land between the girls' and boys' sides. He straddled one of the lines. No one else would take a seat that didn't clearly signify gender. This denial of the male side of the table was an effective message of ostracism. Not only was Michael declared an outsider to the class, he was declared a non-male. He didn't belong with the boys.

It is hard to say how much of the social dynamic a 12-year-old understands. As a teacher, you can control the less subtle forms of abuse: you can stop a fight, you can punish name-calling, you can counsel, you can discuss, you can implore. And yet, in the cracks between, on the recess yard in a silly game of bouncing balls or in the moments when someone chooses where to sit for lunch, the social lessons go on—and maybe they should. Maybe we learn something important. Once you see it, however, it is hard to let go. I kept replaying the choices I made. The intern, who had to supervise the same group at recess, pronounced lunch "just fine," on the grounds that there was no open hostility and everyone ate. As a colleague of mine pointed out when I cornered her at a faculty party and tried to explain the problem, complete with a diagram drawn on a napkin, "It's only lunch." I put away my napkin. I don't do party conversation well. She's right, of course. It's only lunch. Most of us survive lunch.

Sir Judith of the Lunchables™ and the Homework Crisis

When I have a problem, I go and stand in front of one of my bookcases. I think that this is one of the reasons that I like owning a lot of books. Often, I just stare at them. More difficult problems require several bookcases.

The answer must be somewhere in one of these volumes. I scan the subtitles of the *Encyclopedia Britannica, Eleventh Edition (1911): Gig to Har, Ita to Kys, Shu to Sub,* trying to narrow down the categories in my mind. I study the thin spines of my poetry collection where Now *We are Six* sits between *Diving Into the Wreck* and *Omeros.* The short fiction, those under eight inches tall, mesmerize me, but the taller fiction tends to depress me, because I own too many hardcover books I haven't read. I only look at the philosophy section in moments of utter desperation.

I'm convinced that all answers to all questions are somewhere in my small library—I'm just never quite sure of the exact location. I know that the answers are rarely directly related to the topical content of the problem posed. The *Upanishads* have provided marriage counseling; characters from Shakespeare have inspired math problems. *Four Films of Woody Allen* has served as my spiritual guide since I was in college. I have a strange metaphysical notion that we read to find out what we are thinking, not to learn anything from the text, so all books are equally viable repositories for truth. It just happens to be easier to find the answers in some books than in others. I find that my old statistics textbook, for example, rarely proves helpful.

Today, I am searching my shelves for an answer to a riddle. Why have my students stopped doing their homework? Lately, it has become sort of a crisis. I flip through my copy of Kierkegaard's *Either/Or*, noting that there is no physical evidence to suggest that I have ever read this book and hoping something will just pop out at me.

We had begun the year as I begin every year—by discussing why I assign homework. We never talk about it the first week; students need time to do some homework first so that the topic won't be purely theoretical. I pull out the easel, the giant pad of paper, the special smelly easel pad markers, and together we brainstorm a list. The list is, with only slight variations, usually the same:

1. Mr. Goldman is evil and likes to torture students.

2. Homework keeps sixth graders off the streets.

3. Homework keeps kids busy so that they won't watch so much television.

4. Homework provides a chance to practice/review what happened in class.

5. Some types of work are easier to do at home than at school (such as quiet reading).

6. There is more to do than can fit in a school day.

7. Next year there will be even more homework, and students need to begin preparing to handle it.

8. Parents like for kids to do homework because they had to do it when they were in middle school.

9. Students need to prepare so that they can participate in class.

I usually have to prompt them to include the last one. The idea of preparing so that class time can be productive is novel to most students. They assume that the only one who needs to prepare for a lesson is the teacher. Otherwise, the class comes up with the whole list. While all their suggestions

The idea of preparing so that class time can be productive is novel to most students.

might be true, I try to focus them on numbers 4, 5, 6, and 9 because those reasons strike me as most legitimate.

At this point, most students will acknowledge that there are at least some plausible reasons for a teacher to assign homework. A few less, but a good number, will openly admit that there may be benefits to doing homework, in some theoretical, abstract way.

Then, in my best rational, convincing voice I tell them, "You don't do homework for me. I don't need your homework. You do it for the reasons we outlined: it helps you review, it gives you a chance to practice, it helps you get more out of class, and you can get a whole lot more out of this year if you use that time well."

This is a naïve, simplistic, and developmentally inappropriate little sermon, but I can't help myself. Like pasting a warning label on a dangerous product, I feel the need to be truthful about my homework-assigning intentions.

The homework policy itself is pretty simple. If, for whatever reason, students don't have their homework on any particular day, they have to come have a short meeting with me to tell me why they don't have it and when it will be turned in. In my mind, this isn't a punishment; it is simply part of their responsibility as students. Perhaps there is a good reason for missing the assignment. I would consider it disrespectful as a teacher if I didn't listen to what they have to say. Of course, the only time we have for such conversations is during recess, and this makes me a very mean teacher.

One of my strengths as a teacher has always been that I am easily shocked, even in the face of overwhelming contrary evidence. I am always surprised when students haven't completed their homework, even if it has become the norm. Part of me honestly doesn't quite get it. Why wouldn't everyone want to do the homework? This

February, however, even I have to admit that there may be a *reason* students are not doing their homework.

So here I stand at my bookshelf. I have worked myself all the way up to the textbooks I used in my graduate studies. My degree is in educational administration, not classroom teaching, so most of these books have less relevance than the ones on the poetry shelf. But here is Peter Senge's *The Fifth Discipline* (1994), a book I remember liking a lot, even if I cannot recall any of its specific content. I pluck it from the shelf, shoo the cat from my chair, and sit down to read.

························

Lately we have been studying castles. I have given what I see as an interesting and creative assignment. I bring in newspapers, and we spend some time looking at real estate listings—decoding the terminology, noting the sales techniques. I ask each student to compose an advertisement for a castle, appropriate for today's listings but accurate in its details for the time period.

Like many a good idea, this one gets lost in translation. First, I botch the newspaper lesson. My initial explanation of what we are doing isn't clear, and everyone is confused about what they should be looking for. Many of them become so engrossed in reading the paper that the discussion becomes incoherent, and since everyone has different newspapers, we undergo the "not in mine" effect, where no one seems to feel the need to pay attention unless we are discussing his or her particular ad. I become a little frustrated, lose my "isn't this fun" tone, and then spend too long going over all of the project requirements, the grading rubric, the deadlines, and my expectations. By the end of class, no one is interested in this creative assignment, not even me.

When the class goes off to P.E., I pack up my frustrations and go upstairs to the teachers lounge for tea. Heidi, a colleague, listens to my complaints with something approximating patience while she microwaves popcorn.

"They do what they're told," I tell her.

"And that's bad because..."

"I mean they do what they are told to do and that's it. There's no interest, no spark—nothing. They just do what I tell them to do because I told them to do it."

"Except their homework."

"We *have* been having homework problems lately." (This had been the subject of yesterday's whining session.)

"Here's what you do," Heidi explains as she rips open the popcorn bag and dumps the contents in a bowl already too full of old, unpopped kernels for my hygiene standards. "First, you go and buy marshmallows, graham crackers, jellybeans, lots of chocolate, just a whole mess of junk food. You put them in teams, give each kid a pile, and you have them build a castle out of it. Tell them that the castles have to be utterly realistic and show what they learned, blah blah blah. They'll love it; they'll learn something about castles. Done. You need to lighten up."

I'm too horrified to respond, but Heidi isn't waiting for a rebuttal. She takes her popcorn and leaves me standing by the microwave. I have a lot of respect for Heidi. She is a creative, dedicated teacher who has amazing relationships with her students. But I cannot, I will not, sanction candy castle building.

My objection is, in part, simply a question of style. I'm too serious in class but only because I'm too serious in life. Middle school students hate hypocrisy worse than anything else, and they are very good at spotting fakes. This can be limiting, particularly for someone like me who is not a natural performer, has anti-social tendencies bordering on misanthropy, and is really uncomfortable talking in front of groups of people. In Heidi's class, castles with graham cracker drawbridges and marshmallow crenellations might work, but I could never pull it off.

There is also a more basic pedagogical question here. Candy is not a particularly appropriate building tool. In this circumstance, it only serves as a bribe. If I bribe my students to motivate them, I undercut the most basic premise of the lesson—that the knowledge or the skills have value in and of themselves. Learning about castles becomes a mere by-product of candy consumption. I may have motivated students, but I haven't created students who are motivated to learn about castles.

My classroom is, perhaps, unreasonably austere. We don't play games because I don't believe that learning is a competitive sport. There are some opportunities for artistic expression, but not many, because I'm much more concerned with content than presentation. I hate fancy posters with beautiful illustrations and no information. Making Mothers' Day cards is not in the curriculum. In fact, we don't celebrate anything but authentic medieval holidays, which means we will dance around a maypole, but we will not have Secret Santas. We don't make candy castles.

....

All of the students are standing in front of their tables, arms outstretched.

"90°." I bark. They now look like cheerleaders making the letter L.

"45°." The Ls collapse into fallen Vs.

"30°." The hands move a little closer.

We are doing math calisthenics. There is a solid theoretical basis for this drill, involving kinesthetic intelligence and memory recall, but mostly it is a chance to get up and move a little. The same format works well for practicing measurement estimation, plotting coordinates (on tile floors), and learning about rotating objects in space.

It looks a little silly. Actually, it is a little silly. But all of the students do it anyway. The question is, why?

Partly because it's a little silly. There is also, I suppose, an outside chance that I have convinced them of the drill's sound pedagogical benefits. Mostly, however, they do it because I ask them to. This is my classroom; I get to make up the rules.

There are clear, not quite Machiavellian reasons that my classroom has become a monarchy. To begin with, I am the only one who is ultimately accountable. It may be their life, but it's my job. I have to make certain things happen. I have to prevent, to the best of my ability, certain other things from happening. If I have the responsibility, I need the power.

So there are rules, many of them seemingly arbitrary. I don't allow power struggles in my classroom. I always win. It's a rule. In my classroom, no one wears a hat unless they have a note explaining that they are wearing one for religious reasons. All paragraphs have to have at least three sentences. At the end of every school day, there is a price of exit. Usually, they have to tell me something they've learned, but sometimes it is simply a prime number, the spelling of a vocabulary word, or a preposition more than two letters long. If they ask me, I tend to have a rationale for everything I do, but because I enjoy explaining the reasoning and can do it in some depth, most of them stop asking after a while. And that is just as well. I really do have solid reasons for my silly rules, but the single idea that underlies them all is that I want this classroom to feel special.

....

Schools are strange places. Students are sorted primarily by age, sometimes by other factors as well, and the net effect of all this sorting is that they live in a bubble of heterogeneity. There is nothing natural about a room full of 12-year-olds. Eight hours a day, five days a week for most of the year, they sit in desks while some adults (usually greatly outnumbered) make strange, very abstract demands. *Add this string of numbers. Read this story about a girl who lived in the 12th century. Discuss the atomic structure of carbon. Dribble this ball and then throw it at that hoop.* Divining the relationship between these various demands and determining the possible relevance to their pre-teen lives requires an even greater level of abstraction. Some students can parrot the almost reasonable premise that they need the information and skills they are learning now to do well at the next level of their education, but that reasoning only postpones the obvious question: is the whole enterprise valid?

I can't answer that question, although I suspect the answer is "probably not." I can justify what we do only in idealistic terms. I believe there is a value in the life of the mind. Learning is one of the best things about being human—that nearly magical ability to collect and use information, to create new knowledge building on old, to receive the abstracted wisdom of people who have gone before us whom we will never meet. I want a classroom in which we can explore ideas, learn, and grow. A place where numbers count, literature matters, divining the meaning of a poem is an act of exploration. A playground for ideas—a respite from the awful background noise, the incessant shouting of the outside world. In this space, the norm should be that people are nice to one another and work together on common goals. And, since this is not the reason any of my students have arrived in these seats, I, as dictator, legislate it thus. The fact that I am not wholly successful in this endeavor simply demonstrates that there are serious limits to my powers.

....

A small strip of the left side of the blackboard is reserved for the See Me list. In theory, a name written under that heading might mean that the individual needs to come talk to me about any school concern, but mostly it is the list of students who need to see me at recess to discuss missing homework. Katie, my intern, does the actual homework collecting at the beginning of the day, so I never know who will be on the list until she writes it, usually around snack time. Katie is 23, fresh out of college, and far more organized than I will ever be. As the year progresses, she takes on more teaching and planning responsibilities, but we have agreed that she is in charge of the homework. She has a system, and I'm not even allowed to touch the stacks until she gives me permission.

Today the list extends nearly to the bottom of the board. There is an audible break in conversation as everyone looks at the growing column of names. Thirteen. When class resumes, there is a lot of feet staring. Not even the few who did all their homework want to look up and see my reaction.

I don't address the issue, and we have a really lousy math class. Music class takes them away, and Katie hands me the clipboard. Katie's assignment chart is easy to read, so the only question I can think to ask is, "What do you think is going on?" She shrugs and shakes her head.

At recess, the few regulars make themselves comfortable. The procedure is always the same: I start with the students for whom this ritual is a rare event. The ones who miss assignments regularly have figured out that they are not likely to see much recess today.

I start with Brandon. This may be his first appearance on the See Me list this year. I find his name on Katie's chart. Brandon didn't complete his map for geography—a fairly short, rote assignment that we have twice a week. "What happened?" I ask.

Brandon looks up, slightly bewildered as if he himself isn't quite sure. "I spaced the map," he tells me, meaning that he just forgot to do it. "I'll get it to you tomorrow."

"Fair enough. Bye." Brandon shuffles off to recess.

Samuel is next. He is Brandon's best friend and only slightly less consistent about his homework. "I spaced the map too," he offers, a little too enthusiastically. I don't sense conspiracy, but I can guess that he would have had a different answer if Brandon hadn't gone first. I let him go, too.

It takes me almost 20 of the 25-minute recess to work my way down to Caitlin who probably has not brought in all of her homework any day this year. We have been working on her homework issues, but three family meetings later, I haven't seen much of a change. She smiles at me when I ask her what she owes me.

"Math, social studies, and science," she ticks them off quickly. "I did do my map."

"That's a start."

"Long day, huh?" she adds.

"Long day," I agree.

·····································

Sitting in my chair next to the living room bookcase, I skim through the highlighting in my copy of *The Fifth Discipline*. There is a lot of it, which makes me suspicious. Over-highlighting is often a sign that I was trying to stay awake. Senge believes that most people are caught up in linear thinking, when, in fact, "the key to seeing reality systematically is seeing circles of influence rather than straight lines." His book is full of little diagrams of circles with arrows.

I get out my yellow legal pad and my Sharpie markers and draw my own. Here's my homework circle:

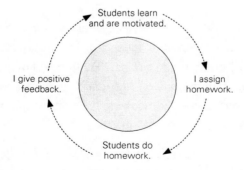

It all seems too simple. Why doesn't it work?

·····································

Because I don't own a television set, I tend to listen to more than my share of radio. I am a bit of an NPR junkie. Today there is another installment in what seems to be an endless series about life in an urban public school. They have covered gang violence, teenage pregnancy, racial tensions, and lack of textbooks. I have yet to hear anyone mention homework as a major issue.

> What distinguishes a class from a collection of adolescents is the degree to which we share a common purpose.

I know that a rash of missing homework assignments is not the biggest problem facing kids this age, even for these students in this admittedly privileged environment. But I also know that what distinguishes a class from a collection of adolescents is the degree to which we share a common purpose. If I can't get them to do the homework, I'm losing them as a class.

According to Senge, "Every circle tells a story." Since I am in a rut, and ruts are linear, the way out must be somewhere in these circles. "By tracing flows of influence," Senge goes on to explain, "you can see patterns that repeat themselves, time after time, making situations better or worse" (p. 75).

....

"Bear with me," I tell Katie as I draw two circles on the easel pad. First, I draw my homework circle. Then beside it, I draw another one.

"See, Senge says that often the manager..."

"We're now managers?"

"Bear with me. You see, the manager often only sees this one circle. See it's a growth cycle because it just keeps just getting better and better."

I trace my homework circle with my marker, showing how the students just keep learning more and more. Katie is being remarkably patient with me.

"But in most systems, there is another circle, a balancing one, and so this process..." I stop and find my page and read: "'runs up against a balancing process which operates to limit the growth. When that happens, the rate of improvement slows down or even comes to a standstill' (Senge, p. 76). So, don't you see? It all makes sense."

Judging by the look on Katie's face, I have overstated my case.

"OK. Let me fill in the other circle." I have already used up a lot of our planning period with this little presentation, so I try to simplify. "The first circle is all from my perspective. The problem is that I imagine my circle as a closed system. When we slow down, I simply push harder on the input—I give more homework and become more insistent on it being done well. If there were only one circle, this pressure should overcome the slowdown. But it doesn't, because there is another circle I have been missing. In this circle, operating from the students' perspective that same input works in reverse."

I add a second circle to my drawing. Katie looks a little puzzled, but not uninterested.

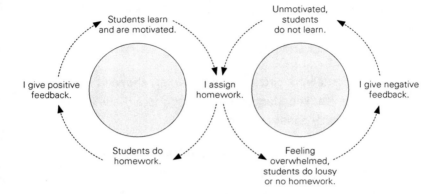

"The circles connect at the point where I assign the work. From there, the students feel overwhelmed and insufficient, do a lousy job, and get negative feedback, which only serves to make them less receptive to the next assignment. The more I push, the more overwhelmed they feel, the quality of the work declines in a vicious anti-growth cycle."

"So what do we do, stop pushing?" she asks.

"Senge says that good managers don't try to change everything, they look for points of 'leverage,' small changes that get at the root of the problem."

"Such as?"

Carl's face appears at the door, several others behind him. It's time for lunch. I flip the cover back over the easel pad. "Not sure," I admit, "but I'm getting there."

When the students enter the classroom the next day, the tables are already set. At each place is a single sheet of paper. At the top of the page is a clip-art knight from a chess set followed by a set of instructions:

> Greetings, Pages of the Sixth Grade. As part of last night's homework, you read about codes of chivalry. What would a Code of Sixth Grade Chivalry look like? Together with the noble youth at your table, I would like you to brainstorm a list of attributes that would describe a true Knight of our Realm (our classroom).

The conversation is unusually lively for such an odd question. I had expected a sort of standard "be nice to each other, do your homework, don't cheat on tests" kind of response, but the word *chivalry* seems to have pushed them to consider broader themes. At least some of them must have done the reading.

We list the attributes on the easel pad. *Steadfastness* makes the list, as does *kindness*, *charity*, and *humility*. No one mentions *chastity*.

"As King of the Realm," I tell them, "I would like to be able to bestow knighthood upon my subjects, but it seems to me that they need to prove themselves first." Our lunchtime reading had been a version of *Sir Gawain and the Green Knight*, so they are familiar with the idea of a quest. At times like this, I wish I were a better performer. There is nothing regal in my bearing or my voice. I had considered a paper crown but rejected the idea as too kitschy.

"Each aspirant to knighthood needs to convince me of her or his worthiness. As you might expect, that convincing has to be written in essay form. As part of that essay, I require three signs or actions—small quests to be completed over the next two or three weeks—that would prove your conviction. Your teachers also reserve the right to make battlefield promotions for examples of extraordinary bravery, kindness, or resolve."

I add one last condition. "Either everyone becomes a knight, or no one. This is a class project, and you need to support each other. Each aspirant's quest will remain a secret," that poor Katie has to keep track of, "and if everyone completes their quest, everyone receives their knighthood."

I have no reason to believe this scheme will work.

At the end of the day, as we set up the classroom for tomorrow, I enumerate the problems to Katie. "There's a good chance that they will just reject the whole thing as being beneath them."

"Maybe."

"And the reward is really vague. Not a party, not a prize, just a title."

"We already presented it to them. You were very excited about it this morning. I think they'll have fun with it."

"It's not supposed to be fun. It is supposed to be leverage."

Katie smiles. "We'll have to wait and see."

When Katie and I sit down to look at the essays, they are better than we could have hoped. The self-suggested quests are both serious and wonderful. Students pledged to become kinder to classmates, volunteer for community service, and help out more at home. One or two students challenged themselves to confront a personal foible—such as shyness about speaking up in class or being less of a gossip. A number of them chose academic proofs of their worthiness including better homework completion. Katie and I select out a few that we think are too ambitious and might sabotage the outcome, but with a little help on the revising, everyone has a quest of his or her own choosing.

....

Katie devises an ingenious method for tracking the quests. We are trying to avoid making anyone into a scapegoat, but we want to keep the students focused on their goals. Katie posts a large blank piece of poster board on the wall above the computers. As each aspiring knight completes his or her tasks, Katie adds a symbol to the display—a star or a shield or some artistic squiggly mark. This way the class can keep count without knowing who has qualified for knighthood. Katie only adds the marks once a day, and it soon draws more attention than the See Me list.

I had proposed the battlefield promotion as a last resort in case someone's quest turned out to be unattainable, but we find good reasons to bestow the honor on several students—all of whom seem pleased when we tell them. It makes me realize that I don't provide that kind of feedback often enough. There are many more opportunities to recognize good behavior than I imagined.

It helps to be looking for it.

"It's working," Katie tells me as she tallies the numbers at the end of the day.

"So far," I admit. "We have a ways to go."

But it is working, or at least something is changing. As I write out each week's assignments, I try to keep Senge's circles in mind, trying to build in a little more flexibility and a little more choice. When I hear myself pushing, I try to ease up, holding firm to expectations but reducing the volume a notch. I do my best to suppress my inner dictator. Caitlin tells me that I seem calmer lately. There are several days when she is my only guest at recess, and a few days when even Caitlin has all of her work, although we never have a day when everyone brings in everything. That might be asking too much.

The Quest Board begins to fill with Katie's symbols. "You know," I tell Katie as I stand in front of it counting, "they aren't learning anything about medieval knighthood from all of this."

"You know," Katie replies, without looking up from her grade book where she is tallying quest completion, "it really doesn't matter."

"Are we just doing our own version of chocolate castles?" I had told her about Heidi's suggestion.

"No, that would have been much too easy."

Two weeks later we hold a knighthood ceremony.

One of the homework assignments this week has been

to choose an appropriate knightly name. In an effort to wring some academic purpose from all of this hubbub, I compile a list of names from the records of English villages in the 12th century, and we discuss the development of surnames. What their own choices lack in authenticity, they make up in creativity—Sir Kian of the Striped Hat, Sir Judith of the Lunchables™. Several of the girls insist on being ladies, not knights, and we let the title be their choice.

Katie and I make certificates on the computer, roll them up, and tie them with ribbon. I bring cupcakes, popcorn, and cookies. It feels like we have something to celebrate.

The night before the event, I stay up much too late writing the script. For each knight I want at least two achievements to announce. At the appointed hour, Katie and I sit formally at the front of the room and call each student forward.

"For your willingness to sit with younger students on the bus and your excellent improvement in Math, I hereby dub thee Lady Catherine of the Freckled Face. For your cheerful disposition and for having memorized all of your lines for the play by the second read through, I hereby dub thee Sir Walter the Point Guard."

It is a very silly ceremony conducted with great solemnity, and yet it is oddly poignant. In the last few weeks, we have turned a corner. I'd like to believe the change came from having the students articulate expectations and set some goals for themselves. That had been my intention.

Maybe the leverage came simply from the energy generated by the novelty of the activity. In February, often *any* change does some good. It is also possible that the improvement in morale had more to do with warm weather and the start of the spring play. I had a colleague who claimed that such shifts are due to sunspot activity—an explanation that works as well as any other. Whatever it was, I had a great opportunity to tell an entire class, honestly, that I was proud of them. They got silly certificates and junk food to eat. The realm survives.

The Problem with Polenta

On the first day of school, Nigel tells me that he is good at math. It's his favorite subject. Nigel is a good-looking young man with a round, almost chubby face that will probably thin out as puberty overtakes him. He is sitting straight in his seat in a way that makes me think of parochial schools. When he addresses me, his mouth widens in an enormous, tooth-filled smile, as if he is angling to win me over. I can't help but wonder if he tells the English teacher the same thing. It turns out he's a little rusty from taking the summer off, but his computation skills are promising if not quite solid. On Thursday, he and the other students are handed the following word problem:

> *Swimming to France*
> I like to swim. It is my favorite form of exercise. This morning while I was swimming, it occurred to me that I swim a lot, but I never get anywhere. What if instead of

swimming back and forth doing laps, I swam the same distance in a straight line?

Now, the pool that I swim in isn't Olympic-sized. You have to swim 72 lengths of the pool to go one mile. I usually swim about 32 before I poop out. I swim an average of three times a week. At that rate, how long would it take me to swim to France?

Now, I know that I can't really swim to France in a pool, but I'm wondering how long it would take me to swim the distance it is from here to France. According to my atlas, the distance from Boston to the closest French beach is 3¾ inches. Boy, France is really close! I know, I know, it is a really bad joke. The distance on the map is obviously drawn to scale. The scale is that 1 inch on the map is the same as 960 miles.

Do not write on this page. Please explain your reasoning clearly and include all calculations on a separate sheet of paper. You may use a calculator if it helps (it may not), but you still need to walk me through all of the steps. Also, make sure you exercise regularly, eat your veggies, and floss your teeth (although none of these are necessary for this word problem).

I explain to the class that the goals of such word problems are threefold. First, I want them to be able to separate the wheat from the chaff, to extract the information relevant to solving the problem. Start by figuring out what the question is actually asking, then what is needed to answer that question. The second goal is to provide a chance to do some good problem solving. The road to a solution should not be obvious, is likely to involve multiple steps and may require trying a number of strategies. Finally, I am interested in how *well-written* the response is.

A good mathematician is able to explain his or her thinking clearly in words.

In fact, the swimming problem is not the best example of this genre. I usually open with it because it has a concrete answer and because I'm sentimental; it is one of the first word problems I wrote.

When I collect the homework the next day, several students have scrawled calculations on the bottom of the handout. I hand those back immediately. The instructions were clear—all responses had to be written on a separate sheet of paper. These are all now redos. Nigel, however, has stapled his answer on a separate sheet. The full page of notebook paper has a proper heading: name, date, and subject. Underneath the heading he has placed four question marks.

....

It is only partly a joke that I communicate to my classes by memo. They are subjected to idiosyncratic instructions, bad jokes, and constant reminders to maintain proper oral hygiene. While I'm sure there is some demarcation separating a language-rich environment from simply drowning in paper, I always have trouble seeing the line. I have begun to hand out fill-in-the-blank forms with my math problems in an effort to elicit longer responses. They have helped Nigel a little. Most weeks, I get reasonable answers to the questions that ask for concrete information, but little or nothing on the back where Nigel is supposed to explain his thinking or to answer the question. When we discuss the solutions in class, he

listens attentively and always says something like—
Oh, now I get it. Maybe he does.

Ketchup v. Missile

Two items in the newspaper caught my attention
recently. One, from an article on boredom, provided
the interesting fact that "when Heinz ketchup leaves
the bottle, it travels at a rate of 25 miles per year."[1] The
other was from an editorial in a monthly intellectual
paper I get, which included a report on the recent test
of an "Exoatmospheric Kill Vehicle," a small missile
designed to shoot down enemy missiles, which missed
its target by six seconds.[2] The vehicle travels at
15,000 mph.

This question has two parts. Please do both.

1. How much faster is the missile than the ketchup?
2. By how many miles did the missile miss its target ?

[1] "Word for Word/Boredom." *The New York Times* (Feb. 20, 2000).
[2] Harris, Bob. "Defense Goes Ballistic." *Funny Times* (Feb. 2000). 2000.

There are several problems with Nigel's response.
To begin with, he has only answered the first question.
He provides the solution: 14,975. As an explanation he
writes: "I subtracted." I ask him to sit down and go over
the problem with me. "So, I see that you subtracted.
Why those two numbers?"

"Those were the only two numbers in the problem."
OK. I point out that both of those numbers are rates, and
we note that one is measured in years, the other in hours.
Nigel looks thoughtful, but doesn't immediately respond.
Finally, he looks up.

"So, should I have multiplied?"

....

Nigel ends up in my creative writing elective. I don't like teaching electives. The only one I've taught that worked well was one on kite construction, and even then, most of the kites fell apart when we tried to fly them. As a faculty, we decided that the electives this term will be more academic. Because I am enrolled in a graduate program for creative writing, I volunteered to do a little seminar on my craft.

There are six students—two of whom are angry because they wanted the drama elective. I start by sharing a little bit about myself as a writer. I bring in my journal. I show them the doodles, the sloppy writing, and talk a little bit about the topics I choose. Class time will be devoted to composing, revising, conferencing with a partner, and workshopping our pieces—all things real writers do. I then hand out the so-called rules:

- All writing must be from your own personal experience. It may evolve from there, but it must be grounded in what you know.

- Poems may not rhyme. Rhyming is too easy to do poorly, very difficult to do well.

- You may not write poems about the following topics: rainbows, sunsets, the glories of nature, or puppy dogs. Poems about cats are acceptable.

Although I get the most complaints about the rhyming and the content restrictions, the first rule proves to be the most challenging for them and the most ethically questionable for me. Encouraging students to see themselves as writers is different than asking them to think like a scientist or a historian. I'm not sure I have the right to ask them to write something personal, but I can't stomach reading the fluff they produce when they don't. So I go for pushing the students to write about their real concerns.

Five of the students write about dating. Four of those ignore Rule Two and produce cute rhymes of iambic pentameter: easy to write, fast to read, nothing memorable. The fifth dating poem has an angry edge that could be developed into something interesting. Nigel's poem is about a trip to Florida. The first stanza sounds like the opening paragraph of an essay that might have the title "What I Did on My Summer Vacation." The second stanza, however, is full of short bursts of interesting images and sounds. He agrees to work some on the poem at home and workshop it next week.

....

His response to the next word problem is, unfortunately, more poetical than mathematical. We had come to The Polenta Problem, from the absolutely true adventures of Mr. Goldman series:

The Problem with Polenta
This is another true story. I was trying to cook some polenta. I copied the list of ingredients below. The recipe comes from a cookbook by Mollie Katzen called *Still Life with Menu.*[1] As you can tell, the recipe book calls for 1¼ cups of cornmeal. I poured the cornmeal

into the measuring cup, and I only had one cup. I still wanted to make polenta. It is a yucky winter night, so I am not going out to buy more cornmeal. I am bound and determined to make polenta with only a cup of cornmeal. How much of the other ingredients will I need to make sure that it comes out edible?

Ingredients:

3½ cups of water
1¼ cups of coarse cornmeal
¾ teaspoon salt
1¼ cups (packed) grated provolone or fontina (optional)

Directions:

1. Place 2½ cups of water in a medium-sized saucepan and bring to a boil. Meanwhile, combine the remaining cup of water with the cornmeal and salt in a small bowl.
2. Add the wet cornmeal to the boiling water, whisking constantly.
3. Cook over medium heat, stirring frequently, for 5 minutes, or until thick and smooth.
4. Stir in the cheese, if desired, and remove from heat.

[1]Katzen, Mollie. 1988. *Still Life with Menu.* Berkely, CA: Ten Speed Press.

This time Nigel didn't bother to fill out the form except for writing his name and the date. Under important information, he writes: "I don't know what polenta is."

"Polenta is cornmeal, Nigel," I explain when we meet to go over his homework. "Tell me why you needed to know that in order to do the problem."

Nigel proceeds through a small litany of gestures. He shrugs, he looks at the floor, he breathes out forcefully, then drops his arms to his side in defeat. "I never know where to start with these things."

We discuss strategies. I give him a highlighter, and he marks the key points as he reads. I have him circle the question and tell me what we are looking for in his own words. In his notebook I have him write a list of possible approaches that he can try when he has no idea of where to begin. As I watch him struggle to decode the list of ingredients, I have the sinking feeling that none of what I offer him will be of much help. There just isn't a magic recipe for solving a complex problem. Nigel tells me his last teacher gave him a list of key words, and he could do all of *her* word problems fine. If the word "difference" appeared in the problem, he knew to subtract. If it said "more," he added. It was like a code, he says. Lots of textbook problems can be solved that way, I thought to myself, yet few real-world questions are answered by deciding which of the four operations to apply to the numbers given.

> I have the sinking feeling that none of what I offer him will be of much help. There just isn't a magic recipe for solving a complex problem.

....

I have now finished writing my recommendation letters for my students. These one-page summaries are incredibly tricky undertakings. The competition to get into the seventh grade programs they are applying for is unbelievably fierce—often, there are only one or two slots available. The schools know me by name, so I have to be honest to maintain any sense of credibility, but I also know that if I include anything that makes the students sound less than ideal, I have nixed their chances. So I go for honest advocacy. I like my students, or at least I try to like most of them, and I can usually find something about each of them that makes me feel comfortable recommending them.

In the special language of schools, words tend to lose their opposites. Students can be *smart* but never *dumb, inquisitive* but not *dull, friendly* but not *mean.* I have lots of students who work *hard* but not one who is *lazy.* Many find certain specific parts of the curriculum *challenging,* but they all are making *good progress.* Nothing is ever difficult, although sometimes students are still *developing a skill.*

I go through several drafts of Nigel's math recommendation. He has performed well on his problem sets, and his scores on tests and quizzes have all been in the top third of the class. Yet I know from the projects and the word problems that there is likely a serious issue with his ability to work abstractly. How well he will do when he leaves me will depend on what kind of a teacher he has next.

I focus on his work ethic:

> Nigel is consistently well prepared for class and
> responsible about his assignments. This steady
> approach works well for him, because it gives
> him the practice he needs and the time to develop
> his skills.

I talk a little about his test scores and how they correlate
well with the results of the standardized testing. I can't,
however, ignore the conceptual issues. I hypothesize that
they are developmental.

> Nigel is just beginning to make the leap to
> more abstract reasoning. He still is more
> comfortable with concrete, computation-oriented
> assignments, but he is learning to express his
> thinking more clearly.

I stare at the letter a long time. I've talked about his
social skills, how well he has adapted to being in a
new school this year. There are a few lines about the
quality of his participation in class. But there is still
something missing…

....

One student is absent, so there are only six of us
gathered around the table when we workshop Nigel's
poem. Everyone listens respectfully—writing workshops
are serious business. Nigel takes an audible breath and
then reads his poem so quickly, he sounds like he was
recorded at the wrong speed. No pauses between the
words, at the ends of lines, not the slightest airhole
between stanzas. If I had not already read the poem
several times, I would have no idea what he is saying. I
ask him to read it again, more slowly. Nigel nods gravely,

composes himself for a moment, and then reads it again at the same speed, maybe even faster. From the look on Nigel's face it is clear that he is not up for a third go-round.

"Would you like someone else to read it for you?" I ask. Nigel nods. "You."

So I read the poem. The compliment round is unusually enthusiastic. Everyone really likes the way Nigel has portrayed the sounds of the beach and the go-carts and the miniature golf. We spend almost the whole period discussing how to convey noises in a poem. Nigel doesn't say much. He looked a little embarrassed by the attention, but he is smiling.

I append one final paragraph to my math recommendation.

> Nigel is in my creative writing elective and was the only student willing to share his poem at a school-wide assembly at the end of the term. I was impressed by Nigel's willingness to revise the piece several times and incorporate criticism. It was a remarkable poem in its attention to details and in the sophistication of its imagery.

Using abstract imagery in a poem is not the same as being able to work on a conceptual level in math. They are arguably separate intelligences. Word problems muddy those waters because they require both mathematical and verbal skills. Nigel suffered through the final term of my word problems without any appreciable improvement, but there was one substantial difference. While he never learned to appreciate the genre, after the elective he was willing to try the problems again—to really try to sort through the language to find the meaning. When I think back on his smile that day, I realize that it was a different smile than the one he gave when he boasted that he was good at math. Fewer teeth were visible, the spread wasn't quite as wide, but something about it looked more genuine to me.

Reflections from Walden Pond

On paper it was a nearly perfect project: student-centered, interdisciplinary, great use of local resources. But, as I watch my band of sixth graders march silently around Walden Pond, the only images that come to mind are those of chain gangs.

This is our third visit to Walden. We have sat on the banks of the pond and written in our journals. Using sterile bottles from our science kit, we gathered water samples to test back in our lab. After reading and discussing selections of Thoreau's writing, we toured the replica of his cabin. The last few weeks of music class have been devoted to practicing choral works based on his prose. Not only have we come to the pond, we have visited a calligraphy exhibit that visually reinterpreted some of his more famous quotations, invited the artist to visit our class, and attempted our own calligraphy. We have employed different modalities, addressed the students' various learning styles, worked cooperatively, and debated our group decisions using all of the best team dynamic techniques. There were structured and less structured activities, concrete and creative approaches, choices and requirements, rubrics and evaluations. And they have hated every minute of it—almost. They like the bus ride there and back.

That's not entirely true. Several students have favorite Thoreau passages, and a few have even memorized some quotations. They may grumble about performing, but they smile when they sing. Some of the poems and stories they have written are quite good, and the discussions are frequently sophisticated and mostly productive. Still...I feel like a failure.

Thoreau describes walking around the pond on a "delicious evening, when the whole body is one sense and imbibes delight in every pore." We might as well be in math class. The students walk, staring at their feet. They don't look at the pond, don't seem to hear the birds. They are obediently silent. The teachers have designated this a silent walk so that everyone can really listen, really observe, really feel what it's like to be here. There was even a discussion about how rare it is in school to give people true quiet time to think and reflect. But no one seems to be enjoying the walk around this peaceful park on this beautiful morning. This is a forced march.

....

I'm trying to remember anything from when I was in sixth grade, but I draw almost a complete blank. I remember incidents from elementary school, and high school is a blur but still somewhat accessible. I know we studied Egypt in fifth grade, and I remember beginning algebra in seventh. I can remember reading Tolkien and The Dark is Rising series, but I think that was earlier. I also know that I had a girlfriend, because we started "going out" in fourth grade and broke up awkwardly in seventh, but I don't remember ever going anywhere with her that year. I'm not sure we even spoke much.

The only distinct memory I can draw from my sixth grade year was listening to the eighth graders who rode my bus talk about my homeroom teacher. Because almost no one in high school rode the bus, the eighth graders ruled the ride home. Only two years older, they seemed to me to be another species. They were taller, louder, and used profanity with a casual regularity. Some sported small amounts of facial hair. Bus coolness was measured by how close to the last rows of seats you could get, and the very last rows were the unchallenged demesne of eighth grade boys. I have had to ride a lot of school buses in the last three decades, and none of this has changed. The code of bus behavior seems to exist independently of geography or time.

Sixth and eighth grade males exist on opposite sides of a biological divide. Neither seem to fit well within their bodies, but the sixth graders are still little boys in spirit and form, while the eighth graders are racing headlong into puberty. This was not the first bus talk I remember about sex. It wasn't the first conversation that referred to the possibility of performing any of a variety of acts on or specific analyses of the female body. What I remember about that bus ride home, however, was that it was the first time I had ever heard anyone discuss a teacher in those terms. The eighth grade boys had decided that our teacher was hot and provided an extensive and detailed appraisal of certain aspects of her anatomy. With no more experience than we sixth graders had, the eighth graders had crossed some border of the imagination that none of us had even dreamed of yet. I listened with a mixture of awe and jealousy. I knew that I was not yet up to talking like that. I assumed that someday I would occupy those seats and command that authority. I was sure I knew how it would feel to be one of them. It never happened, but I can't decide whether that was just me, or if no eighth grade boy is ever as cool as he appears to a sixth grader.

What will the students walking around this pond remember from their year in sixth grade?

The funny thing is that I have no memory of what this teacher looked like. I don't remember her, only that they were talking about her. This one conversation about sex is the sole conscious recollection from that whole year. I know that I learned something in sixth grade. I'm sure I developed essential skills, mastered facts that I still use, grew and changed in important ways. Yet the fact that I can recall nothing specific makes me wonder about the students I'm watching walk around this pond. What will they remember from their year in sixth grade?

I know that it's a false calculus. You don't measure the effectiveness of teaching based on what a student can attribute to a specific learning experience from a distance of 25 years. I also know that I can sing the lyrics to songs I listened to 25 years ago and recount the plots of movies and books I read that long ago. My mother still has some award I won that year in the top drawer of the desk in her living room. She keeps asking me when I want to take it home. I was by all reports a good student. Shouldn't I be able to remember something?

....

For the fourth time this week, Stephanie has stood up and walked out of my classroom. I send my intern after her. We will talk to her, and she will cry or scream at us for ruining her life. I don't believe we have, in fact, ruined her life, but I am beginning to doubt whether we can consider these last few weeks a positive experience for her. I'm pretty sure I can predict what she will remember from this year.

Stephanie is angry because we have, in her mind, crossed a sacred boundary. At her birthday party she had invited several girls to spend the night. Sometime during the evening, two of the girls had helped themselves to some wine that had been left in the refrigerator. The drinking had come to the attention of the school, and the administration had felt that they had the obligation to inform parents of what had occurred. A letter went home.

This, in itself, is a complex, messy situation. But for Stephanie there is so much more to the story. Stephanie is at least two years behind the rest of her classmates in virtually every measurable academic standard. She never does homework, and she does not participate in class. She does not carry on anything resembling an extended conversation with an adult. She shows signs of being intelligent and capable, but she is not able to do any of the required work independently.

I have at least one Stephanie every year. Their histories are always horrific—childhood traumas, witnesses to violence, various medical conditions. Psychiatric files locked away in a special cabinet in the Head of School's office.

I know Stephanie has come an incredibly long way the last few years— academically, socially, and psychologically. I know that we have adapted the program in every way possible to meet her needs, from tutoring to counseling to endless family meetings. I know that even her outbursts are a sign that she is gaining a voice she hadn't had before. I know that I have invested an incredible amount of time, energy, and resources into working with this child. And I know that when I look at her, I don't feel like I've reached her at all, and it isn't likely to get better before the end of the year. You don't keep score in teaching. You don't say, "I did a great job with 18 out of 19." You only mark losses.

I had nothing to do with the letter, the decision, or the open bottle of wine. But in the dichotomy of Stephanie's mind, I am responsible for this egregious invasion of her private life. The actual consequences of the letter are sort of beside the point, both for her and for me. I have become something far more sinister than simply a representative of an oppressive institution. For both of us, I have become the institution itself. Often I am no happier about this transformation than she is.

....

We travel around the pond in three groups, each led by a teacher. As a triumvirate of teachers, we have become remarkably good at making groups. The squads are well-composed. Today, Stephanie is assigned to someone else. This isn't cowardice on my part. I am hoping she might have the opportunity to open up to another adult, since she isn't speaking to me at all. I try whatever I think might work.

I have Thoreau on the brain (clearly some form of disease). In "Civil Disobedience" he writes of the distinction between the individual will and the corporate:

> It is truly enough said that a corporation has no conscience [...] Law never made men a whit more just; and, by means of their respect for it, even the well disposed are daily made agents of injustice. A common and natural result of an undue respect for the law is, that you may see a file of soldiers, colonel, captain, corporal, privates, powder monkeys, and all, marching in admirable order over hill and dale to the wars, ay, against their common sense and consciences, which makes it a very steep marching indeed, and produces a palpitation of the heart.

The path around Walden has no hills. My marchers carry no guns. Still, watching them produces a palpitation of my heart. What am I teaching them by having them hike around this pond?

I often have this same feeling observing them in class. If someone came to photograph them, everything would seem perfect. The students are sitting quietly, albeit somewhat slumped in their seats. Most have the appropriate accoutrements (pencils, notebooks), a few have made eye contact with me, and lots of them can repeat the last sentence I have said verbatim. It's an old student trick. The teacher accuses the student of not listening, and she spits back the last thing the teacher said word-for-word. She hasn't been listening, she has been hearing, but the semantic distinction is never worth arguing. It all looks so right that it is easy to assume the teacher and student share the same classroom.

A few simple tests will show that the appearance is misleading. In my classroom, I assign homework to review concepts, give a chance to practice skills, and extend the opportunities to learn beyond the brief time we have together. In their classroom, homework is something that they are required to turn in so that they don't get punished. With any luck, they may even gain some unspecified reward, although in this ungraded environment, the nature of that reward is a little bit of a mystery. Most of the time, what they produce looks enough like what I expect so that neither of our assumptions need be challenged. Yet, if I ask, almost no one can guess why I assigned a particular activity, nor can they name what it was they were supposed to get out of doing it. In fact, they are a little indignant about the question. I may be able to get them to do the homework (my job), but I can't make them think about it. That assumes that learning is their goal. I once gave the same vocabulary word on my weekly Latin quiz for an entire semester, and I still had students who missed it. These students weren't dumb, they weren't truly apathetic, they just didn't notice. The only way that happens is if they don't see any connection between the quiz and what they are supposed to be learning.

....

Stephanie and I sit in the hallway, mostly not talking. Although we are physically only a foot or so apart, we might as well be in separate rooms. When she finally speaks, she addresses the wall beside her rather than looking at me. "Why are you always asking me how I'm feeling?"

> Although we are only a foot or so apart, we might as well be in separate rooms.

It's a good question. I guess I want her to talk to me. I want to help. All I can think to do at this point is ask her how she is feeling. "It seems like there is a lot going on. I thought maybe you would want to talk about it."

"I don't," she says, still not looking at me. "I'm fine except that I have to come here and have you ask me how I'm feeling all the time."

I am not a psychologist. Stephanie and I have not established a rapport, and she has no reason to trust me with her feelings. But lately she seems to be losing more ground. When I arrange for her to have extra support, either in class or separately, she resents the attention, but on her own there is no way that she can participate. Her aunt, who seems to be the only adult in her life, wants me to address only the academic issues. That would require some semblance of cooperation from Stephanie.

"Not that it matters," the aunt tells me. She has already arranged for Stephanie to repeat sixth grade at a nearby parochial school where they do "lots of worksheets and rote stuff." She promises that she will look into getting some counseling for Stephanie, but it is clear even as she says it that she has no intention of following through. She and Stephanie both believe that I am the problem and that once she changes schools, everything will be just fine.

I send Stephanie back to class and sit by myself for a moment. Am I doing more harm than good with so much attention? Would it be better to let her ride out the year sitting quietly in class, doing no work, pretending that everything is OK? I can't do that, but I also can't convince myself that anything I am doing is helping. Every day, she slips further away.

As cold as it is in Thoreau's woods, I insist on some journal time. Most everybody opts to return to the bus to write, but a few of us sit out in the wind along a low stone wall facing the pond. Ice and patches of snow are still visible in spots. I think it may be colder now than when we visited Walden in December. Facing this direction, the pond seems smaller. From here the wind is louder than the sounds of traffic on route 2A, and with a little imagination one can picture Thoreau puttering along the water's edge. I pull out my journal, but I can't think of much to write. Beside me on the wall, four students sit huddled over their notebooks being far more productive.

On the way home from Walden, the bus gets stuck in the very worst of Boston traffic. We will be late for dismissal, but none of the students seem concerned. They are happily flirting and arguing. The less social are playing handheld video games and listening to music through headphones. I wonder what Thoreau would make of such technology. Old enough to remember a time before kids plugged themselves in for bus rides, I have to admit that I like it. They may be ruining their own hearing, but at least they are sparing mine.

I never know what to do with myself during these interludes. Both of the other teachers have brought papers to grade, but reading in a moving vehicle makes me nauseated. Not that we are moving quickly. Storrow Drive might as well be a parking lot. I ask a couple of the students who are unfortunate enough to sit near me whether they liked the field trip. They appear a little puzzled by the question.

"It was pretty," Olivia offers.

"Pretty cold," Douglas interjects from the seat behind her.

"It was cold," I agree, "but did it help you make more sense out of Thoreau to see the pond? What did you think of the cabin?"

"It was small," Olivia tells me. "I didn't expect it to be that small."

"Anything else?" I ask, mostly addressing Douglas, since he is still looking my direction.

He thinks for a moment, then shakes his head.

....

"I went to the woods because I wished to live deliberately, to front only the essential facts of life, and see if I could not learn what it had to teach, and not, when I came to die, discover that I had not lived." I hated *Walden* when I read it in high school. It felt like the ultimate romantic fluff. Although a nominal Boy Scout, I was not worshipful of nature, and the tone of Thoreau's writing always felt self-righteous and pretentious. Often, for me, it still does. One of the most annoying things about Thoreau is how quotable he is. You can thumb through *Walden* and pick up scores of neat little sayings. Although aphorisms do not constitute philosophy, they have a sneaky habit of lodging in your mind and worrying you like a toothache or a misplaced pen. My sixth graders and I kept coming back to this same line. What does it mean to "live deliberately?" How do we interpret "front" as a verb? How would you discover you hadn't lived if you were already dead?

But it was the deliberateness I felt we were missing. We weren't sucking out "the marrow of life," but letting it be "frittered away by detail." "There is an incessant influx of novelty in the world," Thoreau was telling us, "and yet we tolerate incredible dullness." I am trying my best not to be a purveyor of "dullness." Maybe my mistake is seeing myself as a purveyor at all.

> "There is an incessant influx of novelty in the world, and yet we tolerate incredible dullness." –Thoreau

Our debriefing the next day is more comforting. I start by asking what they remembered about the replica of the cabin. Although "small" is still the dominant adjective, they are able, and willing, to elaborate. For a group that looked utterly bored by the tour, they held onto an amazing number of details, many of which I missed. Maybe I would have noticed more about the house if I hadn't spent the whole time watching them.

I ask for volunteers to read from their journals. Although no one seemed excited to write in them yesterday, almost everyone wants to share what they wrote. The ice made an impression, as did the trees and the few birds. Olivia reads a beautiful description of the sound of the wind.

I am not fooled into thinking that we all had the same experience at Walden Pond or that these journal entries are a sign that my goals for the project were achieved. The conversation we are having in this classroom is still over a divide separating their world from mine, but today the gap seems to have narrowed. Successful teaching is always about finding a way to bridge that gap. Sometimes a teacher can enter their world. I've known some gifted health teachers who can broach very personal topics in real ways, and coaches who talk the same language as their athletes. More often, we teachers drag students into our world by making the stakes feel so high that we all feel traumatized by the need for preparation—whether it is to pass the statewide test or to be ready for seventh grade, or college, or that vague but powerful "success later in life." Sometimes they jump into our world unexpectedly—finding pleasure in a book, revising a poem they really call their own, or asking a real question. Sometimes we find middle ground.

Although it was still chilly by the pond, the calendar claims it's spring. The pond was also icy in 1847 when Thoreau declared that "one attraction in coming to the woods to live was that I should have the leisure and opportunity to see the Spring come in." For me, with my years always starting in September and ending in June, the seasons reverse their connotations. Unlike Thoreau, I dread spring. Fall is the season of hope, of rebirth, the start of the world from the desolation of August when all planning is merely theoretical. I always begin September full of energy, ideas, and confidence. But spring is the Sunday evening of the school year—the time when I am facing the things I put off all weekend, realizing that they won't be done by Monday. By spring, I am cutting my losses. Faculties discuss next year a lot in the month of April, because by

March, this year feels done. The kids have one foot out the door, and everything is a struggle. And yet, maybe not too surprisingly, it is often in the process of separating that we draw closer together.

> It is often in the process of separating that we draw closer together.

Susie, the music teacher, has somehow arranged for the spring concert to take place in Faneuil Hall. It is a majestic venue with huge historical paintings behind the stage. As the students receive their preperformance instructions, Susie takes a moment to point out the portrait of George Washington standing next to the back end of his horse. There are several copies of this painting around Boston, and she wonders aloud what the artist might have been suggesting about our first president by presenting him this way.

The sixth grade has brought along the posters showing our research into pollution at Walden Pond and copies of our literary magazine that includes a number of Thoreau-inspired poems. There isn't really a good place to set up the displays, and we end up propping them up on some chairs to the side. This may be just as well, as our results are dubious at best. One group's measurement of contaminants showed a puddle in the street ten times cleaner than the pond.

The performance is a much bigger success. The sixth grade's choral interpretation of selections from *Walden* is the finale, following a mélange of songs and dances by the younger students. My class is not nearly as cute as the first grade's crowd-pleasing rendition of a Scottish folk tune (something about crows), but they sing well and receive a warm round of applause.

Stephanie doesn't sing. Susie requires everyone to stand in proper performance position but always gives the option of standing silently. Sometimes the non-singers look defiant, but Stephanie looks more lost than anything else, as if she isn't sure how she got here and what is going on. She smiles slightly when the crowd applauds.

"I left the woods for as good a reason as I went there," Thoreau writes in the conclusion to Walden. "Perhaps it seemed to me that I had several more lives to live and could not spare any more time for that one." The little house by the pond was just one step on his journey, and there came a time to move on.

On the second to last day of school, the students write postcards to their future selves. I will mail the cards in late August so that they arrive during their first week of seventh grade at their new schools. I know that writing them is a cathartic experience for the students, but I've never asked what it feels like to receive one in the mail. They also write notes to each other, which my intern and I turn into giant Goodbye Cards. I learned early on never to let them write notes directly on the cards because someone will write something that will ruin someone's card, and it will precipitate a crisis. They write on labels. Even though I tell them that I will read and edit, I still get questionable results. Several of Stephanie's labels contain references to her efforts to drive me into retirement. I let those pass. Douglas has to redo several of his because they include lines like "Thanks for French kissing my girlfriend right in front of me. I guess that's what best friends are for." At least it gives me an opportunity to have a nice chat with him about the pains and trauma of adolescent social life.

Before we go to their graduation ceremony, I make it clear to the students that there are two things they are required to do before they leave. They may already have their diplomas, but they must take home their final portfolios and their cards. And they must hug me goodbye. It is a mandatory hug, no exceptions. It saves both of us the awkwardness of deciding whether it's OK. They all do it, even Stephanie—although, technically, it is more of a lean than a hug. I stand there with my pile of portfolios growing smaller and watch them leave one-by-one.

They walk away, some holding a hand of a parent, and now they really look like the little kids they are. They climb into cars and disappear. I'll see some of them again—they'll stop by or I will run into them at a T-stop or at the movie theater. Sometimes, depending on whom they are with, they will acknowledge that they know me. Some of my earliest students are now well out of college. I know a few are teachers—at least two now teach sixth grade. Even as I watch this class leave, I'm planning new projects for my next one, sure that this time I might get more of it right. They are leaving; I don't seem to be going anywhere soon.

The Bus Ride to Straight Culture

Shayna takes the chalk and her turn at the board. She writes out her full name, Shayna Stiller Abrams, in large letters at a good 45 degree angle. This is one of those multicultural exercises I learned at a workshop, and I am using it as an icebreaker for my new sixth grade homeroom. So far it hasn't been inspiring. The students are supposed to introduce themselves by explaining the origin of their full name. A few students know something about how their names reflect their family's ethnicity, but we have had way too many my-parents-just-liked-its and I-don't-knows, and I am beginning to think this has all been a waste of time. Joy was named for the dishwashing soap and Ashly's mother thought she was being original by leaving out the "e," but in terms of revelations, this has been a bust.

Shayna explains that her first name is Jewish and that she is part Jewish, although she's not sure what her name means. She's pretty sure it means something; she just can't remember what. Stiller is the last name of one of her mothers; Abrams is the last name of the other. She gives a little shrug at this and hands off the chalk to Eleni, who isn't at all sure where her name came from, but knows she doesn't like it.

Bone-thin with long, dark hair, Shayna is a quirky and intelligent girl, given to reading fantasy novels rather than doing all of her homework and more comfortable stretched out on the couch playing cards at recess than running outside. She is cheerfully disorganized, but she manages to do enough to avoid getting herself into trouble. Her sole political act is to campaign endlessly against my no-hat rule, devoting several essays and a few acts of civil disobedience to the cause. But Shayna knows the line between mischievous good humor and disrespect and never crosses it. During the year she will undergo the usual traumas of being a 12-year-old girl: fights with her best friend, arguments with her parents, some adolescent romantic angst.

Shayna has handled this little presentation at the board with a calm assurance born of repeated practice. When I ask her whether this exercise was comfortable, she laughs. "I have been a poster child for two-mother families since I was six," she confides with an impish smile that belies the maturity of her tone. "Nobody much gives me trouble about it." Shayna is my first student with two mothers, but she will not be my last. Over the next few years, I will have a handful. After that, I expect to see a lot more.

Issues of race, gender, sexual orientation, ethnicity, and socioeconomic status all matter in a classroom. How could they not? As teachers, we talk a lot about educating the "whole child," forgetting that this totality includes aspects of the student that might we be less comfortable talking about. I pride myself on treating each student individually, taking each one for who he or she is. But who they are has to include where they come from, what their families are like, what issues they face on the subway ride home as well as in my classroom. Do I therefore treat my black students differently than white students, the wealthier differently than the kids on free lunch, the children of divorce differently than those with two parents at home? Does the fact that she has two mothers change the way I teach Shayna?

The simplistic answer is yes and no. If I treat all of the African American students the same, I am being racist. If I treat all of the students with gay parents the same, I am acting in an equally discriminatory manner. But I think it is also harmful to pretend that all the students are essentially alike, as if they just happen to come in different designer flavors. I need to treat Shayna differently because she's Shayna, not because she has two moms. I am comfortable with this stance in theory. In reality, the dynamics are often more subtle.

....

I am on the phone with a parent when Hannah comes racing into the teachers lounge frantically looking for me. The three flights of steps have winded her, and she looks even more disheveled than usual, her coat hanging from one arm and her hair suffering from the static effects of her recent de-hatment. Ms. Pierce has sent her up to find me, she explains between gulped breaths, because Cameron stomped on Skyler somewhere he shouldn't have, and she needs me to come to the recess yard. I don't ask where Cameron should have stomped on Skyler but follow Hannah down the stairs.

Ms. Pierce has Skyler sitting up. He is crying but looks more angry than hurt. I send Cameron into the library to wait for me; the librarian will keep him busy until I get there. Ms. Pierce takes the rest of the class back to our room, mouthing, "Math notebook corrections?" to me. I nod. Quiet, focused work seems like a good call for the moment. I sit with Skyler, listen to his side of this story, and then help him to his feet. The nurse has him spend the next 45 minutes with an ice pack on his privates, which strikes me as medically unsound, but he returns to class reporting that he feels better.

Cameron waits for me in the small tutoring room off the library. He is a short, intense, frequently funny kid who has textbook Attention Deficit Hyperactivity Disorder (ADHD). Even medicated, he is prone to outbursts and impulsive actions, but his honest efforts to control his behavior and his willingness to work with his teachers make him so likeable that I would never describe him as a difficult student. Cameron has made a lot of progress this year, both academically and socially. He writes amazing poetry, retains discrete facts with astonishing accuracy, and excels at math. He has also been kicked out of P.E.

multiple times, spat in the holy water when we visited a church, and now has stomped on Skyler.

Cameron cannot explain to me what happened. They were sort of play-wrestling—the popularity of the WWF wrestling has encouraged a lot of that this year—and then Skyler was down on the ground when Cameron jumped on him. Somehow, the play-acting had given way to actual physical violence, but Cameron isn't sure why. He will admit that he doesn't like Skyler, but he hadn't really meant to hurt him; although, he can see now that stomping on him there would be painful—"It happened really fast."

Cameron's parents will be brought in for a conference with the school head, and after a lot of discussion, he will end up serving an in-school suspension. Cameron will feel appropriately remorseful, but at no time will we address what is at the root of this problem. Although this will be the worst of the incidents surrounding Skyler, it has not been, nor will it be, the only one. Like Cameron, Skyler is funny, personable, and medicated. Skyler is on antidepressants, and his problems are frighteningly complex: his parents are threatening divorce, he has been diagnosed with obsessive compulsive disorder, and he might be a rare male anorexic. He is, without a doubt, one of the brightest kids in the class, but he is barely performing at a sixth grade level.

Skyler is different from his peers intellectually, socially, and psychologically. Different is always difficult in middle school. The one trait, however, that seems to attract the most attention from his classmates is his femininity. There is something in his speech and his mannerisms that they describe as stereotypically gay. They don't always use that word, nor do they appear to fully understand what they are reacting to, but their impersonations and their teasing focus almost entirely on this aspect of his persona. If Cameron had attacked Skyler because he thought Skyler was gay, this would be a hate crime. But neither Cameron nor Skyler seems to think of it in this way. What looks like prejudice to me, looks like just another fight on the playground to them.

Blatant discrimination is fairly easy to address. As a class, we have several discussions devoted to an outbreak of using the word "gay" disparagingly as a synonym for anything that is mass-culture popular without being acceptable—mostly movies or songs by boy bands. The discussion becomes a learning experience, and we can refer to our class charter, which prohibits any kind of discriminatory language. Several students equate misuse of the term "gay" with racial epithets, and there is widespread agreement around the

Outlawing bigotry is not the same as providing acceptance.

table that, even if the intention wasn't to put down gay people, it still showed prejudice. Shayna participates in the discussion, as does Skyler. Everyone seems comfortable. The tone is warm, accepting, and serious. I think these discussions are helpful and reaffirming, but they only address overt issues. I'm not sure they do much for students like Skyler. <u>Outlawing bigotry is not the same as providing acceptance.</u>

•••••••••••••••••••••••••••••••••

"David is gay. He told me at lunch." So begins the second chapter of my novel, *Two Parties, One Tux, and a Very Short Film About the Grapes of Wrath* (Bloomsbury, 2008). The novel centers around a friendship between two high school juniors; one gay, one straight. When people ask why I decided to write a YA novel, I tell them it was my homework assignment, which isn't quite true, but almost. One of the classes I took in graduate school was a fiction course called Writing the Young Adult Novel. On the first day, we were asked to write a description about an incident from our own adolescence. I wrote about the night my best friend, Bert, told me he was gay.

I had not set out to write a novel about someone coming out, but my professor and the class liked the topic, and a novel began to take form. Although there isn't much of Bert or me in the final draft, the emotional core of the novel drew heavily from that experience. That night marked a kind of a turning point in my life. Before that night, I did not know anyone who was gay. In 1981 in North Carolina, it was nearly unimaginable for a high school student to come out. Even telling someone you trusted was a huge risk. I remember telling Bert I didn't think he really was gay and that, even if he was, it didn't matter. I was wrong on both counts.

Bert, it turns out, was and is gay. He knew. When I told him that it didn't matter, what I was trying to say was that we could still be friends. I wasn't lying. We are still friends more than 30 years later. But it did matter that he was gay in ways I didn't quite get. It was pretty easy for me to say it was OK, but it was a lot harder for him to reconcile who he was with the world he lived in. I remember him trying to explain. "You don't understand," he told me. "Every song on the radio, every television show I watch, every movie I see tells me that there is something wrong with me." He might have also mentioned the church he grew up in; his parents, who would spend the next 10 years sending him letters about how he was bound for hell; and the grandmother whom he would never tell, but his point was more about culture. "You and I don't live in the same world. You live in a world where everything you see confirms something fundamental about you, and I don't."

It is not enough simply to fail to perpetuate discrimination.

As a teacher, I often think about Bert's description of what I had assumed was a shared culture. I am a straight, white male—traits that I don't believe should bar me from the teaching profession yet don't add much to the diversity of a teaching staff. I can loftily ban prejudice; but for my students to feel at home, it is not enough simply to fail to perpetuate discrimination. In some way, I need to expand the culture of my classroom.

My workshop on multiculturalism had also encouraged us to examine our assumptions. Part of the problem with assumptions is that often you don't know you are making them, so they tend to be hard to examine. I had already done the easy things. Our classroom library included books with gay and lesbian characters. Our human sexuality curriculum was inclusive. I had abandoned the set of grammar worksheets I once used, because all of the examples were built around the stereotypical dad-mom-two kids-and-a-dog family and replaced them with my own slightly idiosyncratic versions. I think these were good steps, but I'm not sure they made much of a difference.

....

Shayna enters the classroom in tears. Tears are a little too common in sixth grade for this to signal a real emergency, but tears at 8:10 in the morning are usually a bad sign. While Ms. Pierce collects homework and starts our morning routine, I ask Shayna if there is anything wrong. This is a pretty stupid question, but Shayna nods solemnly, and we go sit in the stairway to talk. This upper flight of stairs leads to the administrative offices, so students don't regularly need to use them, and lately these few steps have become my unofficial conference room. They provide a small measure of privacy without the tension of sitting in an office behind a closed door. The school is housed in a pair of turn-of-the-century brownstones, so it is big on charm but not always an ideal space for children. This stairway is drab, dusty, and smells like shoes, but I'm thankful for it anyway.

I did not think ahead to bring a box of tissues. Shayna uses her sleeve to wipe her eyes and nose, and I pretend not to notice the line of snot on her jacket. I ask again if she's okay, and she says "Yes, just upset." I ask if she wants to talk about it, and she shakes her head. We sit for a while in the dank staircase. Finally, she explains that she doesn't really want to talk about it because she doesn't want to get anyone else in trouble, and then the conversation quickly becomes a guessing game. She seems willing to provide yes and no answers.

"Did something happen on the bus?"

Shayna nods yes.

"Was there some sort of fight?"

Another yes.

"Physical or words?"

"Words," she says, gaining a little confidence.

"Inappropriate language?"

Another affirmative nod.

"Name calling?"

This line of questioning eventually dissolves into the full story. Maria, a fifth grader, has been accusing Shayna of being a lesbian. Shayna is very clear that her mothers are gay, but she isn't. Maria and Shayna know each other from an after-school program they both have attended for the last few years. There has been tension between the two for a while. Over the course of the day, I will have separate conversations with both girls and then a long session with the two of them. In the end we reach a sort of truce. Tonight I will be on the phone with both sets of parents.

On the face of it, this is a clear case of the kind of intolerance we have been trying to prevent. But nothing is ever that simple. Of all the girls who could attack Shayna about her sexuality, Maria's motive is the most complex; she comes from a two-mother household as well.

Maria defends herself by stating that she doesn't see anything wrong with being a lesbian, therefore it isn't name-calling. She says she wouldn't care if Shayna had accused her of the same thing. It is a hollow defense—but it illustrates the crux of the tension. At home the word "lesbian" is simply descriptive and even something to be celebrated. At school, it is still and insult. Both girls live in two worlds, each with slightly different rules and expectations. On the bus, riding into straight culture, Shayna's sexuality is an issue, and Maria knows it. Whether Maria is using it to deflect attention from her own family or simply to attack Shayna for some other reason, the difference in the two worlds leaves Shayna, despite all her confidence and support, still vulnerable.

One of the hardest things about teaching is that most of the learning happens in real time. You don't get to meet your students, get to know them, go home and study for a few months, and then come back to teach them. Creating a classroom environment in which every student could be comfortable was not a one-time fix; it was something I would struggle with year after year.

Shayna was my first student with two moms. It would be a few more years before I had my first student who was openly gay. I am still learning what it means to talk about transgender. When I began teaching, I didn't think much about what kinds of families my students came from. I guess I just assumed I knew what a family looked like. But my families and my students are not all the same and that is O.K. In fact, it is more than O.K., it is wonderful. Because some of those families bring me students like Shayna.

Swimming Lessons

It is 8:45 on a Tuesday morning in July. The auditorium has just enough seats for the 215 students and the four dozen or so staff in our program, but, despite a series of whiny memos from me, the adults still prefer to stand on the sides rather than sit with their classes. Some battles you won't win. I take a deep breath, hold up my hand, wait for the shooshes and then the quiet, and welcome everyone to the assembly.

This is my third year with this project, an after-school and summer program sponsored by a private foundation. We work with students who show academic and personal potential and have expressed an interest in attending Boston's elite public exam and independent schools. Although our admissions policy is not race-based, our mission is to open up opportunities for students who otherwise might not have them, so our students tend to come from parts of Boston where many of their friends won't even finish high school. They are economically, racially, and ethnically underrepresented at the schools they will apply to. The foundation provides logistics, counseling, and a 14-month academic program designed to compensate for the disparity between the expectations of the schools they are leaving and those of the ones they hope to attend. In math, that can be a three-year gap, in English, sometimes even more. Socially it can be vast.

During the summer I run what is essentially a small school: a full day, a full slate of academic subjects, homework every night. Ours are the kind of students that teachers dream about. They are willing to invest their time and energy into what they do. They are excited about learning and thrive on challenges. They are in this un-air-conditioned building in 90-plus-degree heat. This is motivation.

Several times a week the whole school gathers together for a tradition called a faculty talk. At these assemblies, some faculty member is strong-armed into giving a short speech on a subject of interest to him or her. In theory, these talks are inspirational—stories about climbing mountains, being the only girl on a high school wrestling team, reconnecting to a grandmother's past by visiting her birthplace. My favorites are usually the ones that deviate from the script. One faculty member lugged in a box of his favorite books and told what he liked about each one. Another brought her seventh grade school picture, in which she sported a particularly humiliating haircut. Today, it's my turn. This is my third talk. As one of my colleagues notes later, each of my talks has shared the same theme. All of them have been about failure.

When I was eleven, I tell the students, I was on a swim team. This wasn't a nationally competitive team. It wasn't even a school team. My family belonged to a local pool, the Westwood Swim Club—six lanes and three tennis courts with a view of I-40. Westwood competed against other local pools. Membership at the club was the sole requirement for making the team.

We practiced five days a week at 8:30 in the morning. The water was always cold. Swim practice, as far as I can remember, consisted almost entirely of swimming laps. Sometimes I think we practiced shallow dives off the starting blocks, but what I mostly remember is swimming laps. We did a lot of them.

Our meets were every Saturday for most of July and August. On Thursdays we had time trials, a sort of internal meet to determine who would represent the Westwood Swim Club on Saturday. There were four different races for my age group: freestyle, backstroke, breaststroke, and a relay. Boys and girls competed separately. For each meet we needed two boys in each of the first three races and four boys for the relay. Theoretically, there were ten slots, but often the same boys would swim multiple races. Whoever placed first and second in the time trials swam that race on Saturday. The first four finishers in the freestyle made up the relay team.

So there I stood: a skinny, short 11-year-old. Every day I showed up for practice. I swam my laps. I pushed myself. I was determined. I was disciplined. And I was unbelievably slow.

Every Thursday, Steve Deal and a sidekick of his, whose name I can't recall, magically appeared. They were also 11, but they didn't look 11 to me. They were taller, more muscular—I think Steve already had hair on his chest. They don't bother coming to practice the rest of the week. Every Thursday, they beat the swimsuit off me and went on to race on Saturday. July and most of August passed by, and I never made it into the top five.

But I was a good team player. I showed up at every Saturday morning meet and cheered my swim mates on. I jumped up and down when we won, looked appropriately despondent when we lost. And every Monday morning I was back in line, shivering in the early morning breeze, waiting to do more laps.

I knew I would get my chance. When it came, I was ready. At the second-to-last meet of that summer, one of the other teams didn't bring enough swimmers, which left an extra lane open. We weren't allowed to have three boys compete, but the coaches agreed that an "exhibition" swimmer could swim in the free lane. Guess who got to be the exhibition swimmer? Anyone else would have been embarrassed to swim in that lane, but not me. This was an opportunity. I didn't expect to win; all I wanted was the chance to be part of the game.

I lined up on the blocks. I did my shallow dive and took three strokes before my first breath. I didn't watch anyone else; you never look at your competitors. I was all concentration. Here was my chance, and I gave it everything I had.

It was a two-lap race, up and back. By the time I made it to the end, the next group of swimmers was lined up on the blocks, impatiently waiting for me to finish. The other boys who swam in my race were nowhere in sight, already out of the pool and toweled off. At least they hadn't started the next race. Actually, I'm pretty sure they couldn't because they needed my lane. Nobody said a word when I pull my exhausted body from the pool.

So, why do I tell this group of highly motivated, high-achieving students this pathetic story? I guess there are several lessons I hope they might learn from it. The first one is that sometimes it is hard to tell what it might mean to win. As an 11-year-old, I did not feel like I had won that race. I felt no pride climbing out of the pool, and nothing anyone could have said would have made me feel better that day.

But in retrospect, this was not a bad experience. I'm now close to 40, and I swim three days a week. My alarm goes off at 5:30 each morning so that I can be there when the pool opens at 6:00. The water is still cold, and I still do laps. I'm still slow. What I learned that summer about swimming had nothing to do with that race. I learned to play a sport that I still enjoy. What more could I have asked for? I don't know what happened to Steve Deal and his friend, but I wonder if they still swim.

We constantly tell kids they can achieve whatever they want to achieve. We tell them stories about Michael Jordan not making the basketball team in junior high and about Olympic athletes overcoming everyone's doubts to be gold medal winners. We love to tell about underdogs. What bothers me about these stories is not the veracity—some are undoubtedly true. Nor am I finally concerned that for each of these successes there are lots of abandoned dreams—stories we don't tell. What I find disturbing in these homilies is the emphasis on winning as the desired outcome. All of the stories end the same way: Keep trying, and eventually you come out on top.

> What I find disturbing in these homilies is the emphasis on winning as the desired outcome. All of the stories end the same way: Keep trying, and eventually you come out on top.

When we focus on achievement, we lose the value of failure. If I had been a great swimmer, maybe nothing would have been different. Maybe I would still get up early in the morning and do laps as an adult. But if I had been a good swimmer, I think I would have come to believe that I practiced so that I would win races. If that proved true, my understanding of the activity would be fundamentally different today.

Having done my best to convey how utterly mortified I was when I crawled out of that pool as an 11-year-old, I go on to tell the assembly about how, a few years back, I would go swimming at a local YMCA three mornings a week and how, each time, the same guy would be in the lane next to mine. This man was easily in his 70s. He had short, white hair and plentiful wrinkles, and he swam almost twice as fast as I did. I could tell, because he would regularly lap me. I have to stop here and wait for the giggles to die down.

What is wonderful about that fact, I tell the audience, is that it really doesn't matter. I am no longer in a race. I swim because it makes me feel good. When I exercise regularly, I tend to skip meals less often, feel more alert during the day, and sleep better at night. Exercising in the morning also clears my mind. I do some of my best thinking while I'm doing laps. Nothing I get out of the activity of swimming changes when someone does it better than I do, even if the guy is almost twice my age.

This is a lesson that took me a long time to learn. And it is an even harder one to teach.

Around the same time I was being outswum by that old man, I was teaching a section of fifth grade math. The school believed strongly in tracking students, and these students had spent the last five years in "standard math" instead of the faster-paced "enriched" or "accelerated" (there are no "smalls" at Starbucks). For convenience, these groups had been labeled A, B, and C—standard being C. One year, they were labeled X, Y, and Z—standard being Z. (How's that for ego building?) I changed my group designation to G (for Goldman), but the composition remained the same regardless of the name. Confidence for this group wasn't high. They knew who they were.

Metaphors can make all the difference. As long as we see curriculum in its etymologically correct sense of a race, then we will evaluate students on how far and how fast they have run it. My fifth graders probably were not destined to complete AP calculus by the time they finished high school. If the purpose of my math class was to push them a little farther on the road to calculus, these students were wasting their time. Other people, like the septuagenarian swimming next to me, would finish faster and do more.

We are only wasting our time if we see curriculum as a race.

The flaw in the race metaphor is that the value of learning math does not reside in the completion of calculus. Even if we are in the same pool, we don't have to be in the same race. There is a lot of great math that these students could encounter, a lot they could learn that might change their understanding of the world and—odd as it may seem— have practical application in their lives. I would go as far as to say that almost none of the benefit one might get from taking math depends on the speed with which you complete it, or how old you are, or whether you end up taking the most advanced course offered. We are only wasting our time if we see curriculum as a race.

I don't tell all of this to the assembly. I hope that the story of the speedy septuagenarian is a strong enough fable that it might resonate for a while, and maybe the students can make some connections on their own. Half of them are probably thinking, *what a loser*. So be it. But to be a loser, there has to be a race. The second lesson I learned from swimming, I hear myself telling them, is that school and life are not races.

At the end of every faculty talk, the speaker has to take a few questions. I get asked whether I still see that old guy every morning, and I explain that I no longer swim at that pool, but I hope he is still going strong. One student wants to know whether I stayed on the swim team, and I briefly recount my sports history. I gave up the swim team for the diving team. Then I played basketball, soccer, and finally, in college, lacrosse. And no, I was never much good at any of them. What they don't ask is whether, if I had the chance to replay that event, I would rather win the race—or at least not embarrass myself so badly. I'm not sure how to honestly answer that one. I'd like to think that I wouldn't.

This is the implicit third lesson of my talk, and it is a little trickier. The real moral of the story is that it is possible to try your best, work your hardest, give it everything you've got and still fail. I tried lots of sports, some with outcomes that make my swimming story look positively uplifting. Someday maybe I'll tell them about how I struck out at T-ball or fell off the board at my first diving meet. The truth of the matter is that sometimes you lose. But here's the kicker: failure, the kind of failure where you have done your best, is a good thing.

Testing a hypothesis and putting oneself on the line requires an emotional readiness to take a fall. The most important skill students can develop is the willingness to put themselves on that line again and again. As in any martial art, learning to fall without causing oneself permanent damage requires practice.

I watch the students file out of the assembly and go to their classes. We are late. No surprise. I have talked longer than I was supposed to. They were a great audience. They looked engaged, or most of them did—there will always be one or two who nod off. And it has been shown in study after study that people retain almost nothing of what they hear, even when they are listening. I know that it is quixotic, at best, to imagine that I will change the way these kids see their education in a short talk at one of hundreds of assemblies they will be subjected to in their lives. The importance of failure is a hard sell to anyone, particularly students like these, for whom success seems so promising and easy to define. They do well in their classes and soon will attend the very best schools in the city. They will win awards, scholarships, and recognition. I did, too, but that isn't what I tell them about. I'm sure I learned a lot from classes I aced. But there is also a lot to be learned from being a lousy swimmer.

Define Teacher

I am standing in a classroom in front of a small table on which I have placed some measuring cups, a stack of carefully taped together note cards, two spoons, and a cruet for salad dressing. These are my props. I am about to teach a lesson on ratios. In some ways this feels very familiar. I am comfortable with the topic. Measuring cups and note cards are among my favorite props for illustrating math concepts. Nevertheless, I'm nervous, and my hands feel sweaty. I'm nervous because although this is a classroom, and I am teaching math; at this moment I am not a math teacher.

School doesn't start for another week. There are no students here. I am surrounded by a circle composed of the faculty of my school and a smattering of administrators. Today I am not teaching a class, I am in charge of a full-day staff retreat. And I have chosen to have the teachers spend the entire day learning about ratios. I have reason to be a little nervous.

....

I began my teaching career as a Latin teacher, but not because I wanted to teach Latin. Sometime during my senior year, I read an article by a former president of Haverford College who offered the following career advice: Whatever you wake up in the middle of the night and say, "That's what I'd like to do," *that* is what you should be doing. All through my senior year, I waited for inspiration. I met with a career counselor who set me up in front of a computer that was supposed to analyze my skills and preferences. It suggested that I become either a mail carrier or a movie director. After graduation, I moved in with some friends and got a job waiting tables. Then one night, mid-summer, I woke up with the thought that teaching might be fun. That was the entire content of the epiphany. Not that teaching would be fulfilling or that I would be a good teacher. No sense of service or mission. Just that it might be fun.

I hadn't studied education, but many private schools are willing to hire liberal arts majors without experience. In fact, I had several friends who already had teaching jobs. With the goal of becoming an English teacher, I registered with a teacher placement agency. However, Latin was undergoing a revival in the late eighties; there was a shortage of Latin teachers, and my degree was in Classics. Although Classics is usually defined as Latin and Greek, I only did the Greek half. So, when the agency sent me to interview at schools, I repeatedly had to explain that while I would be willing to teach AP Latin, it would involve me teaching at a higher level than I had ever studied. I kept suggesting that I would make an excellent English teacher. Finally, in late June, a desperate headmaster brushed aside my pesky objections. After all, I knew Greek, and this was just middle school Latin. He figured I could keep at least one step ahead. The big question was whether I could handle an eighth grade homeroom. I took the job and spent the summer studying Latin. I wanted to teach.

....

According to the National Education Association, 20% of teachers leave the profession in the first three years. I was almost part of that statistic. In September of 1990, the beginning of my third year teaching Latin, I submitted my resignation effective the following June. It wasn't that I hated my job, quite the opposite. I had grown to love Latin. I had favorite Latin poets and spent my summer reading Cicero. And I really loved teaching. I hadn't, however, really decided that I wanted to be a teacher.

We live in our verbs, but we don't use them well. We always ask kids what they want to be when they grow up, when it seems that we should be asking about what they will do. They can't answer "be smart." But mostly, adults want nouns, not verbs for answers. Lawyers don't really law; no business person businesses; architects and contractors don't architect or contract. There are verbs like doctoring and engineering, but doctors practice medicine and engineers design things. When we ask kids what they want to be when they grow up, we are revealing a truth that they don't yet know. We don't *do* our professions—we become them.

The stacks of graded quizzes, the hours of listening to students read the text haltingly, the projects and the note cards, the banquets where we wrapped sheets around ourselves and pretended they were togas—all of the daily stuff of teaching Latin—had slowly transformed me. When I left that job, I wrote in my journal, " I am taking with me none of who I am here." The who I was there was a teacher. Two years later I was back in the classroom.

....

Although this is the first retreat I have been asked to run, this is my second year at this job. I am now a math coach. Now I see students only indirectly. My main job is to work with faculty on planning, assessment, and curriculum development, which explains a little about why we are spending the day on ratios. But oddly, I am not actually trying to teach about ratios. The goal of the lesson is to understand ratios, but the goals for the day don't even mention the word. My goal for the retreat is to begin the long, slow process of changing the way we think about teaching math. Ratios are a means to that end. I am now deep in the world of meta-education.

The day starts out pretty well. I have enlisted the music teachers for the setup. We gather in a circle, and they announce that they have commissioned a new school song. Then, with completely straight faces, the music teachers sing the name of the school to the tune of "Hot

Cross Buns." There is a moment of genuine horror before everyone realizes they are joking.

A good project has a hook, a setup, and then a clear goal—a challenge that must be completed. The song is the hook. The setup, in this case, is several boxes of junk. On the tables at the end of the room I have arranged stuff that I hauled out of my basement—scraps of wood, PVC tubing, old Tupperware, bottles and cans from my recycle bin, string, tape, rubber bands, and assorted clips. It looks like a table of junk because it *is* a table of junk, and almost all of it really did come out of my basement. I invested $1.34 in some extra wood and a little extra PVC tubing, because my kids had claimed most of the smaller pieces.

And now the goal. "Before we leave today," I tell the teachers, "you have to use this junk to make an instrument capable of playing our school tune—"Hot Cross Buns." Tomorrow we will give a concert on our instruments for the music staff." Everyone turns and looks at the piles of debris on the table. The reaction, needless to say, is not overwhelmingly enthusiastic.

·····································

When I first started coaching, I tried modeling lessons in teachers' classrooms, but it never worked quite right. Even when I managed to pull off a reasonable lesson, it felt incomplete. Teaching math well is not about following a script or saying the right things. To have class go well, you have to establish relationships, know the kids, know what they need, and create the circumstances for them to go about learning it themselves. I don't model lessons well—there isn't much value in observing me "doing a lesson." All of the critical work is in the thinking, the planning, and the preparation. The result of all that cogitation is often something simple and direct, but it works because it is the right activity for the right students at the right time. It is good teaching but a lousy show.

To have class go well, you have to establish relationships, know the kids, know what they need, and create the circumstances for them to go about learning it themselves.

My current solution is to try to teach teachers in the same way I would teach students. I try not to be condescending; I teach the way that I would like to be taught—but I teach, I don't model. Today I am teaching this group of teachers about ratios. For some it is review, for others it is something they may have learned once but don't remember. As a school, we span a wide age range, so I have pre-kindergarten teachers in the mix who probably thought they would never have to face an equation again once they left grad school. We will stop and discuss the choices I have made in my planning and what kinds of assessments I am using as the day progresses, but they are not here to observe me teaching. They have to make instruments, and they will have to perform on them. To make the instruments, they will have to know a little bit about Pythagoras and the relationship of lengths of strings and tubes to the sounds they produce. They will have to experiment. They will measure megahertz on their iPhones. They will have to learn about ratios.

About halfway through the morning, I will make them create snack mixes out of bulk- size containers of cheese balls, chips, and pretzels. Inevitably, one group will choose to organize everything in a 1:1 ratio. I will have to ask them to challenge themselves a little more. It isn't that different from teaching sixth grade.

....

I often tell people that I became a math teacher because of a scheduling mistake. After my first teaching job, I worked in the credit and collections department of a phone company. My job was to call small businesses and try to convince them to pay their bills. Along the way, I learned how to do word processing and make spreadsheets. One of the schools I applied to picked up on this experience and asked me if, in combination with a lighter Latin load, I could also teach a computer class. It wasn't that long ago, but in computer time, it was the Stone Age, when the idea of teaching kids something other than programming was still new. I accepted. As a computer guy, I was now part of the math department. A week before school started, some staffing changes resulted in a single fifth grade math class that had no teacher. They asked me if I could fill in, and I said I would. As a new teacher who hadn't even officially been added to the payroll, what else was I going to say?

I still thought of myself as more the English teacher type, but no one had hired me to teach English. As it turned out, I ended up having more fun teaching math that year than I did teaching anything else. In the beginning, I thought I knew fifth grade math—after all, I had always been a pretty good math student. But being able to do fifth grade math is not the same as being able to teach it. I might have been able to divide fractions, but I had no idea why it worked to multiply by the reciprocal. I could find an average but was stuck trying to think of why a fifth grader should care about averages. I spent hours relearning fifth grade math. Not pedagogy—math. Whatever success I had that year was due to one thing: for the first time in my life, I was honestly excited about all the different ways numbers worked. I remember a moment when I had written $a \times b = b \times a$ on the board and was struck with how truly magical that idea was. I had known the rule for decades, but it never seemed beautiful before. What began as a compromise to fill a hole in the schedule became an opportunity to explore another whole realm of knowledge. I was on my way to becoming a math teacher. By the time I switched schools again, I was hired primarily to teach math. The school didn't even have a Latin program.

....

We have about half an hour before we break for lunch, which is a tricky time of day. The morning has gone well, but much of it was exploration. In small groups, the teachers had made discoveries about music and ratios, and now each group has hung a poster for the others to look at. I have done my little mini-lesson on ratios, and they had practiced with the snack activity that gave me a chance to see if they got it. I love food as assessment.

But now I have to pull it together, and the truth is that the information on the posters isn't exactly what I was hoping to see. The data is a little hard to interpret, and the connections are going to be hard to make. And it is close to lunch, which is a really lousy time to keep a class's attention, even if it is a class of teachers.

I bring out my ukulele and I strum a few chords. When I announce that I am not going to sing about ratios, people look relieved. Instead, I use it to illustrate the concepts that are on the posters: the relationship of string length to sound, the specific ratios that produce a tune, the fact the same ratios work even on different length strings. I am getting nods and some good questions; we can safely go to lunch.

As I repack my ukulele, I receive a compliment: "I had no idea that you had a background in music. This is really a wonderful synthesis of music and math."

I don't have a background in music. I know about ten chords on the ukulele, and I have never taken a music course. Three weeks ago, I had no idea what the "Pythagorean Comma" was nor any knowledge of the physics of notes, except a vague memory that there was some experiment you could do with string. I didn't know how to make a trumpet out of a hose or that the number of megahertz is inversely related to tube length. I had to learn everything the teachers were learning today. I just had to do it before they did.

···

I did get the chance to teach English. After years of being a closet writer, filling up my journals with stories and poems that sat on shelves in my study, I decided to go back to graduate school for an MFA in writing. I justified it in my mind by telling myself that it would open up new opportunities for me. I was thinking high school English teacher. But the real motivation was the weight of all that writing sitting on my shelves. It had reached a significant enough mass that I couldn't pretend it was something I did just for my own amusement. I had stories that I wanted to make into published books, and I didn't know how to get them there. While earning my degree, I taught composition and research writing to undergraduates. We read novels, and they wrote papers. Each instructor had to pick a theme for the freshman writing course. One class studied the novels of Don DeLillo, another looked at death as a theme in 20th century literature. My class focused on food. College students love you if you bake them cookies.

I learned a lot that year about food, about novels, about college students, but the most startling thing I learned was that there wasn't anything all that different about teaching English. What I liked about teaching English was exactly what I liked about teaching math. Or Latin. Or computers. I like the endeavor of learning new things as part of a group.

···

It is mid-afternoon and the teachers at the retreat are having a blast. They are hammering nails and sawing plastic bottles apart. They are blowing into tubes and making rude noises. I knew from the time I spent trying out this project with my kids that there were at least six different instruments that we could make out of the junk, but the faculty has come up with several I had not thought of. I begin to relax a little. There was so much that could have gone wrong. No one in this room is a full-time math teacher, so there was the chance that my ratio lessons would be intimidating. We seem to have survived that. There was the chance that the project could have been too easy, and everyone would have immediately figured out the magic ratios and made the instruments. They didn't. My biggest fear was that it wouldn't feel relevant and that this group of busy teachers would resent being made to do math all day instead of having more time in their classrooms or time to argue about the schedule. No one appears to be angry about how we spent the day. It is beginning to look like everyone in the room will make at least one instrument that fulfils the requirements. Wow.

I have been thinking about what made this project work. In part, it was because I put a lot of time into the planning. I had to do research and try out various ideas to find ones that would work. I practiced. I made lots of instruments. I rehearsed my mini-lesson on salad dressing in front of my wife, who duly noted that I reversed the proportions of vinegar and oil. It was also the right project for the day. I had considered having them do a sort of scavenger hunt of Boston or even the newspaper building project I used to do with my sixth graders, but those didn't seem to fit who they were. We are a school that tries to incorporate music into all aspects of our curriculum, so the connections felt right. As a small faculty, we see each other a lot but rarely get to work together on a project. The active problem solving, the cooperative learning, a tangible outcome all seemed appropriate. Mostly, I wanted us to do something that, at first, seemed ludicrous and later felt like an accomplishment. Building instruments out of junk seemed likely to fit that bill.

In the end, however, I think part of what made this project work is that I found it compelling. I got to learn new stuff. I could convey excitement because I was amazed that you could take three pieces of PVC tubing, and simply by cutting them in certain ratios and then hitting them with a flip-flop, produce a song. It wasn't that the idea was so original. You can find hundreds of music and ratio activities on the Web, but I don't think that if I printed out one of those, it would have been successful. This project worked because it was truly mine. Yes, I stole bits and pieces of it from lots of different sources, but what I ended up doing in that classroom was pure me.

....

I believe we are living at a time when teaching is being radically redefined. The pressure on teachers has grown enormously. It is palpable; you can feel it when you visit classrooms. We still may talk as if the students and all of their individual concerns matter, but, as a system, we have reduced them to a set of numbers, and we have reduced the job of teaching to producing those better numbers. As districts and administrators chase those scores, they have latched on to predefined practices that have been, in some way or another, shown to be effective. Where there used to be many ways to teach math, there are increasingly right and wrong ways. The right ones are the ones that produce the scores.

> We have reduced students to a set of numbers, and we have reduced the job of teaching to producing those better numbers.

When I started teaching, textbooks were sets of problems. Now they are almost always scripted. You can open to page one on day one and simply follow the instructions. The next day, turn the page, and there is your next lesson. Everything—games, tests, letters to parents—it's all included. It is a complete package. Insert teacher here.

Increasingly, school is becoming a system of modular parts available for purchase. There are reading systems, science modules, social studies units. There are companies that provide you with everything you need for assessment including tests, scoring, suggested lessons, and handy reports you can send home. There are some wonderful programs that train teachers how to manage their classrooms or how to talk to kids about bullying. But the net result of so many programs, systems, and modules is that they disempower teachers. The experts are now out there, and they can tell us the right and the wrong way to do all of those things we have come to call teaching. If I am judged on how closely I conform to the right models and how well I implement the right systems, then I have no more decisions to make. I am no longer a teacher but an implementer of someone else's ideas, someone else's curriculum, someone else's protocol for my morning meeting and for conflict resolution. I think it is significant that we don't often talk about teaching teachers. We use words like *train* or *develop*. You train someone to implement a program. You develop people for a task. Learning is something students do. As adults, we aren't required to be learners.

I have been following a lot of the arguments about how to evaluate teachers, in part, because my current job is to support teachers so that they can achieve their accountability goals. Many of the criteria that have been suggested make sense: Depth of knowledge about your subject, evidence of planning, solid classroom control. These lists are constructed by trying to distill the essence of what makes effective teachers effective. The rubrics can run to pages and can be quite specific: displays learning targets in the room; uses positive language to correct mistakes; displays student work. I think of myself as a pretty good teacher, but I'm not sure how well I would score. Often I have had to develop my knowledge of certain subjects as I went along. I never have been good at bulletin boards. I try to reach all

Good teachers bring who they are into the classroom, and that is what works.

of my students, but the truth is that certain kids do really well with me, and others don't. But what really strikes me is that the teachers I have known over the years whom I consider to be real superstars, would score even worse.

I think it is OK for us to try to define good practices and encourage good teaching. We have a lot to learn from experts and from each other. But in the end, I don't think you can reduce what makes a good teacher to any one list. Good teachers bring who they are into the classroom, and that is what works. I think the thing I bring that is most powerful is simply a true love of learning. I like to learn new things. It may be the only consistent theme of my career.

....

It is now almost 4:00. The teachers are sitting in a circle, each holding onto something that can reasonably be called a musical instrument. There is a trio of zither looking things to my left. We have tiny tube trumpets and water filled flutes. One teacher has constructed a cool pan pipe, but blowing on it is irritating her bottom lip (I should have brought more sandpaper), so she is playing it by tapping it with a small metal rod. One of the administrators is holding a part of an aluminum downspout covered with rubber bands. As we go around the circle every group is able to play the required three-note song. We rehearse for tomorrow's performance, and it sounds truly dreadful, since each instrument is only in tune with itself. There is a lot of laughter. I take a deep breath. It feels like the right start for a new school year.